Spotlight on Young Children and PLAY

Each issue of *Young Children,* NAEYC's award-winning journal, includes a cluster of articles on a topic of special interest and importance to the early childhood community. Most of the selections in this book originally appeared in *Young Children,* vol. 58, no. 3, in the cluster "Play for All Young Children." Others come from books published by NAEYC and from Beyond the Journal (www.naeyc.org), an online collection of resources that complement and expand on articles found in the journal.

Cover photos © Ellen B. Senisi except as follows: *(front cover)* top left and photo below it © Tovah P. Klein; top right © Jonathan A. Meyers; bottom left © Lynn Bradley; *(back cover)* bottom left © Elisabeth Nichols.

Illustrations throughout ©Thelma Muraida.

Through its publications program, the National Association for the Education of Young Children (NAEYC) provides a forum for discussion of major issues and ideas in the early childhood field, with the hope of provoking thought and promoting professional growth. The views expressed or implied are not necessarily those of the Association. NAEYC thanks the contributors.

ISBN 1-928896-16-2
NAEYC #284
Library of Congress Control Number: 2004105545

Printed in the United States of America

Contents

Spotlight on
Young Children
and PLAY

I fell in love with the E.E. Cummings poem "in just spring" when I was old enough to know that play was for little kids but still a free spirit who wished she could play hopscotch and jump rope forever.

in Just-
spring   when the world is mud-
luscious the little
lame balloonman

whistles   far   and wee

and eddieandbill come
running from marbles and
piracies and it's
spring

when the world is puddle-wonderful

the queer
old balloonman whistles
far   and   wee
and bettyandisbel come dancing

from hop-scotch and jump-rope and

it's
spring
and
   the

      goat-footed

balloonMan   whistles
far
and
wee

— E.E. Cummings

I can picture "eddieandbill come running" and "bettyandisbel come dancing." They are having great fun and, if I look closely, learning to count and think and compromise and appreciate the mud and puddles of the natural world.

As early childhood educators, we know that children learn through play and that the skills and knowledge gained through play are wide ranging. But play also fills children with wonderful feelings. Long after the play ends children still hear the whistles of the "goat-footed balloonMan."

I asked my colleagues to share their memories of play—What did they play with? Who were their playmates? Where did they play? Here are some of their responses:

"In Trinidad we set up a 'dollie house' in the gallery—what you would call a porch. We pulled the yellow centers out of hibiscus blossoms to make cheese and served it on little plates."

"I had a small, soft hairbrush with a handle that became anything I wanted it to be—a car, train, or truck rolling up and down the arms of a chair or across the floor."

"As the children of academics, we tended to create elaborate play

Illustration and adaptations throughout © Thelma Muraida

scenes—library, school, hospital, and restaurant. My sisters, who grew up to be librarians, and I invented a system for cataloging and lending books."

"There wasn't much for a young child to play with on my grandfather's farm. One afternoon, in the dirt of the back yard, I converted a small rivulet of water into a pretend river with buildings along its banks. I spent hours totally engrossed in play."

"Outdoor play is what I remember most. Although our parents had given us a backyard playhouse, we preferred to spend hours building a fort. Because we lived on the water, swimming, splashing, and playing with sand and clay filled many days. Rocks along the shore were ruined castles or mountains to be climbed."

"Our neighborhood gang liked to roller skate, play jump rope, and slide down a dirt hill. And our backyard log cabin got lots of use as a setting for all kinds of pretend play."

"Our upstairs hall was long and straight, with a carpet running down the middle. On either side were two ideal paths for rolling marbles. We spent hours playing a made-up game we called marbly-peg."

There are common threads in these recollections. We played alone, with siblings, or with friends. Playthings were found objects or toys that wore out before we tired of them. Outdoor play featured prominently, as did building, making up games, and pretending. And the play was fun, engaging, and, although nobody mentioned this, filled with opportunities to build social and physical skills while solving problems, reading, writing, and keeping score.

The articles collected in this book focus on the varied powers of play—as a source of enjoyment and as a tool for learning.

In "Chopsticks and Counting Chips: Do Play and Foundational Skills Need to Compete for the Teacher's Attention in an Early Childhood Classroom?" **Elena Bodrova** and **Deborah J. Leong** describe how teachers help children engage in the kind of play that prepares them for future academic challenges.

"The Bugs Are Coming! Improvisation and Early Childhood Teaching," by **Carrie Lobman,** compares play to improvisational theater. Lobman describes how teachers can engage toddlers in improvisation and help them take their play to new levels.

Jane P. Perry, author of "Making Sense of Outdoor Pretend Play," explains how, in her program, the outdoor play yard sets the stage for types of pretend play that are not likely to take place indoors.

In "Choosing Play Materials for Primary School Children (Ages 6–8)," **Martha B. Bronson** provides a chart listing a plethora of materials for various types of play that support and nourish children's development.

"Playing to Get Smart," a viewpoint by **Elizabeth Jones,** provides a series of play vignettes and discusses how and what young children learn through play.

"Play: Children's Context for Development," by **Tovah P. Klein, Daniele Wirth**, and **Keri Linas,** is an overview of the unique characteristics of play.

In "Thanks for the Memory: The Lasting Value of True Play," **David Elkind** summarizes theories of play and reminds us that play is fun and an essential part of a healthy life.

"Helping Babies Play," by **Janet K. Sawyers** and **Cosby S. Rogers,** gives us ideas for helping babies from birth to 18 months explore their world.

In chart form, "Play Modifications for Children with Disabilities," by **Susan R. Sandall,** offers practical suggestions for modifying the curriculum to ensure that all children have opportunities to engage in play.

Diane E. Levin's "Beyond Banning War and Superhero Play: Meeting Children's Needs in Violent Times" invites readers to consider ways to accommodate children's need to make sense of their real-life and media experiences with violence.

Ingrid Chalufour, Walter F. Drew, and Sandra Waite-Stupiansky's article, "Learning to Play Again: A Constructivist Workshop for Adults," offers a practical guide for conducting a dynamic, hands-on workshop to reacquaint adults with the principles and value of play.

— Derry Koralek

Chopsticks and Counting Chips

Do Play and Foundational Skills Need to Compete for the Teacher's Attention in an Early Childhood Classroom?

Elena Bodrova and Deborah J. Leong

For the Chinese New Year, May's parents had given her some sweets to share with her classmates at snack time. "Let's play Chinese restaurant," suggests the teacher after the children finish their snack. Children run to the housekeeping area and start emptying the cupboards. "But we don't have any Chinese food," remarks Taylor, examining plastic hamburgers. "No chopsticks," says Nita, holding up spoons and forks. "Can you pretend you have them?" asks the teacher. "How about using pencils as chopsticks and counting chips as food?" "No, I want to play family," answers Nita, settling into the familiar routine of stirring a pot as Taylor begins to place plastic hamburgers on the plates.

What is happening here? Why don't the children engage in a new play scenario? Should we worry about these children's apparent lack of pretend play skills, and if so, how can teachers intervene?

These might not be the most burning questions on the minds of preschool and especially kindergarten teachers. In an age of rising expectations and tougher academic standards, educators are more likely to pay attention to issues that seem to be more closely related to school readiness. "I used to have a lot more play," sighs a kindergarten teacher, "and now my principal

Elena Bodrova, PhD, is a senior consultant at Mid-continent Research for Education and Learning in Aurora, Colorado, and a research fellow at the National Institute for Early Education Research. She has more than 20 years of experience applying Vygotsky's theories in early childhood classrooms, focusing primarily on play and early literacy.

Deborah J. Leong, PhD, is a professor at Metropolitan State College of Denver and a research fellow at the National Institute for Early Education Research. Debbie has written about early childhood education assessment and prekindergarten standards, and she codeveloped the Tools of the Mind Research Project.

Photos courtesy of Elena Bodrova except as noted.

does not understand why I want to keep the playhouse in my room. She thinks children should play at home and come to school to learn."

Why play belongs in the early childhood classroom

Would you agree with this principal's position? At first it does make sense—many preschool and kindergarten programs run for a half-day only, and spending time on play seems like a luxury. Maybe home *is* the place where play belongs. In our own memories we see ourselves spending a lot of time playing with our friends, and most of this play did take place outside the classroom. At that time it never occurred to teachers that they should provide any kind of support for children's play—it was taken for granted that most children knew how to play, and those who did not would learn from other children.

These nostalgic memories are probably the reason some teachers and school administrators are reluctant to consider play as important a part of the classroom as other activities. However, when asked to describe how children play

Nowadays young children spend less time playing with their peers and more time playing alone, graduating from educational toys to video and computer games.

today, most educators agree that play has in fact changed from what it used to be 30 or even 20 years ago. Nowadays young children spend less time at home playing with their peers and more time playing alone, graduating from educational toys to video and computer games.

When they do engage in sociodramatic play, children rarely try a new theme, preferring instead to act out the familiar scenarios of family, school, and doctor. Even books and TV shows filled with information about realistic as well as fantasy settings and characters often fail to inspire children to turn the housekeeping area into a space station or animal hospital. Teachers (as well as families) comment that today's children tend to rely on realistic toys and props, and they have a hard time using their imaginations to invent a substitute for a prop they do not have. Children often resort to repeating aggressive actions over and over again instead of developing involved play scenarios.

"What a wonderful castle!" exclaims the teacher as she admires a structure Esai and Spencer have just completed in the block area, "Do you want to play knights and dragons?" continues the teacher, reminding the boys about the book they read in class. "I see you have enough knights in your castle, and it is strong enough to protect them from the biggest dragon." The boys seem puzzled. "We don't have any dragons," says Esai after a long pause. Spencer looks around to see if there are some dragons. He glances at the science area where numerous boxes of plastic dinosaurs and crocodiles are stacked under the reptiles poster. He looks back at the teacher. "No, we don't have any dragons," Spencer says.

The home and classroom experiences of many children may not be sufficient to produce the rich, imaginative play that has long been considered an inherent characteristic of early childhood. Many factors contribute to this state of affairs:

• changes in the social context (children spend more time in the company of same-age peers who as play mentors may not be as effective as older siblings or friends);

• increasing academic demands of preschool and kindergarten programs; and

• the tendency of toy manufactures to produce ever more realistic playthings.

To combat these negative factors, early childhood teachers would need to support play development at least at the same level as they support the development of fine motor skills or phonemic awareness. But it is hard to expect all early childhood teachers to follow this advice because, outside of the early childhood community, play is not universally recognized as a medium for learning.

"I am finding myself between a rock and a hard place," admits a former preschool teacher who now writes

© BmPorter/Don Franklin

books for the parents of young children. "Because I work for a publishing company, I need to meet the demands of our customers. However, being an early childhood educator, I know that if I write only what is in demand, it would not be right for the children. All parents want now are worksheets, and they want them in their babies' hands as early as possible."

In practice, the need to promote foundational skills, such as phonological awareness or listening comprehension, in young children and the need to support their play appear to be competing for teachers' time and attention. But in theory it should not be this way. Research on play accumulated over the past several decades makes a convincing case for the benefits of supporting high-quality pretend play. A number of studies show the links between play and many foundational skills and complex cognitive activities, such as memory (Newman 1990), self-regulation (Krafft & Berk 1998), distancing and decontextualization (Howes & Matheson 1992; O'Reilly & Bornstein 1993; Sigel 2000), oral language abilities (Davidson 1998), symbolic generalization (Smilansky & Shefatya 1990), successful school adjustment (Fantuzzo & McWayne 2002), and better social skills (Corsaro 1988).

In many studies focusing on the relationship between play and literacy, play interventions resulted in an increase in children's use of literacy materials and their engagement in literacy acts, as well as gains in specific literacy skills such as phonological awareness (for a review of the research, see Roskos & Christie 2001). Not only does play help children develop skills and concepts necessary to master literacy and math, it also builds the foundations of more general competencies that are

> **Studies show the links between play and many foundational skills and complex cognitive activities, such as memory, self-regulation, distancing and decontextualization, oral language abilities, symbolic generalization, successful school adjustment, and better social skills.**

necessary for the children to learn successfully in school and beyond.

Considering what we know about the effects of play on young children's learning and development, the disappearance of play from early childhood classrooms looks even more alarming. With opportunities for children to engage in high-quality play outside school becoming less and less common, early childhood teachers may soon be children's only play mentors.

The task of supporting play while making sure children meet school expectations may seem impossible, especially given the constraints of a typical early childhood program. However, we believe it can be done.

During our years of work with preschool, Head Start, and kindergarten teachers, we found that knowing the characteristics of high-level play and being able to support those characteristics not only results in richer, more imaginative play but also has a positive effect on the development of foundational skills, including cognitive and emotional self-regulation and the ability to use symbols. These foundational skills in turn make it possible for children to achieve higher levels of mastery of specific academic content, such as literacy (e.g., Bodrova & Leong 2001; Bodrova et al. 2003).

The Vygotskian approach to play

Our analysis of play is based on the works of Lev Vygotsky and his students (Bodrova & Leong 1996; Bodrova & Leong 2003). While Vygotsky's views of play are familiar to the Western educational community (e.g., Berk 1994; Berk & Winsler 1995), the work of his students—Daniel Elkonin in particular—is relatively unfamiliar in the West.

Elkonin [1904–85] is known in the United States primarily through the use of Elkonin Blocks in Reading Recovery and other remedial reading programs. In Russia, Elkonin's research (1978) on phonemic awareness is only part of his legacy; his study of play is another substantial contribution to the field.

Having studied learning in primary-grade students and younger children, Elkonin was a strong opponent of lowering the school-entry age in Russia. He argued that not only would it not help increase student achievement, it would also result in pushdown curricula and the elimination of play from the lives of preschoolers and kindergartners. As an alternative he developed a highly successful curriculum for the primary grades that allows elementary school teachers to teach all requisite skills and concepts without adding more academic content to the existing preschool and kindergarten curricula.

Elkonin identified four principal ways in which play influences child development. All four expected outcomes of play activity are important for preparing the foundations for subsequent learning that takes place in primary grades (Elkonin 1977, 1978).

1. **Play affects the child's motivation.** In play, children develop a more complex hierarchical system of immediate and long-term goals. In fact, play becomes the first context in which young children demonstrate their ability to delay gratification—something preschoolers are known to struggle with in most other situations.

2. **Play facilitates *cognitive decentering*.** The ability to take other people's perspectives is critical for coordinating multiple roles and negotiating play scenarios. Assigning different pretend functions to the same object involves cognitive decentering. This newly acquired competency will later enable children to coordinate their cognitive perspectives with those of their learning partners and teachers. Eventually this ability to coordinate multiple perspectives will be turned inward, leading to the development of reflective thinking and metacognition.

3. **Play advances the development of mental representations.** This development occurs as the result of a child separating the meaning of objects from their physical form. First, children use replicas to substitute for real objects; then they use new objects that are different in appearance but can perform the same function as the object prototype. Finally, most of the substitution takes place in the child's speech with no objects present. Thus the ability to operate with symbolic substitutes for real objects contributes to the development of abstract thinking and imagination. (It is important to note that Vygotskians believe that imagination is an expected outcome of play, not a prerequisite for it.)

4. **Play fosters the development of deliberate behaviors—physical and mental voluntary actions.** The development of deliberateness in play becomes possible because the child needs to follow the rules of the play and because play partners constantly monitor each other to make sure that everyone is following the rules. At first, this deliberateness is demonstrated in physical actions (for example, a child moves on all fours when playing a cat or stays still when playing a guard), social behaviors, and changing speech registers in language use. Later, this deliberateness extends to mental processes such as memory and attention.

According to Vygotskians, only when these four outcomes are in place can a young child profit fully from academic activities. If these foundations are missing, the child may experience various difficulties adapting to school, be it in the area of social interactions with teachers and peers or in the area of content learning.

The kind of play that helps children develop all four foundations is defined by a combination of the imaginary situation children create (the scenario), the roles for people and perhaps objects, and the rules about what players can and cannot do in the scenario (Vygotsky [1966] 1977; [1930–35] 1978). Outside the Vygotskian framework, this kind of play is often labeled sociodramatic play, role play, or pretend play to distinguish it from other playlike activities, such as stacking blocks on top of each other or playing games.

By the time children turn four, they are capable of engaging in this kind of complex play with multiple roles and symbolic use of props. However, in reality many preschool- and even kindergarten-age children still play at the level typical of toddlers, spending most of their play repeating the same sequence of actions as long as they stay in the same role. We use the term *immature play* to distinguish this play from *mature play* that should be expected of older preschoolers and kindergartners. Although mature play does in fact contribute to children's learning and development in many areas, immature play does not provide these benefits.

It seems to us that in many instances when parents or school administrators propose replacing play in an early childhood classroom with more academic activities, they are prompted by the fact that the play they see in these classrooms is actually happening at an immature level. It is hard to argue for the value of play that is repetitive and unimaginative.

Following Vygotsky's principle of learning leading development (Vygotsky [1930–35] 1978), we designed a system of interventions to scaffold play in children who for some reason did not receive adequate support for their play at home or at school (e.g., Bodrova & Leong 2001; Bodrova et al. 2002). Each strategy targets one or more characteristics of mature play. This article shares some of our insights into how early childhood teachers can promote mature play.

Helping children create an imaginary situation

When children create an imaginary situation, they assign new meanings to the objects and people involved. As a result, they practice *operations*

> **A**n advantage of these nonspecific props is that children must **use more descriptive language** when interacting with their play partners.

on meanings that are mentally more sophisticated than operations on real objects. It is apparent, however, that the cognitive benefits of engaging in imaginary actions depend on the kinds of props and toys children use: realistic and specific props do not require a great deal of imagination.

A good way for teachers to support the development of imaginary situations is to provide multipurpose props that can be used to stand for many objects. For example, a cardboard box could be a computer in the office, a sink in the kitchen, or a baby crib for a doll in the nursery. An advantage of these nonspecific props is that children must use more descriptive language when interacting with their play partners: unless they describe what the object stands for and how it will be used, the other children will find it hard to follow the change in meaning of the object from one play use to another.

Another alternative to providing realistic play props is to encourage children to make their own. For example, instead of using plastic hamburgers and fried eggs in a pretend restaurant, children can make their own play food with playdough and other art materials.

Some children may not be ready to make their own props or to play with unstructured objects. They will not play unless there are some realistic props available. For these children, teachers need to introduce symbolic use of objects gradually—both in the play area and outside of it. In the play area the teacher can start with realistic props to keep play going and then add other materials that are increasingly less realistic. For example, a pretend grocery store can combine realistic props (grocery cart, scale, cash register) with some that are generic (boxes, plastic bags) and some that are open ended (pieces of paper that can be used for play money, coupons, or shopping lists).

Outside the play area, teachers can use additional strategies to help children create and maintain an imaginary situation. These can be used during group time or in a center with four or five children. For example, teachers can show the children common objects and brainstorm how they can use these things to stand for something different: a paper plate looks like a Frisbee to one child, a flying saucer to another, and a pizza to yet another.

After all the children learn how to transform real objects into pretend ones, the teachers could extend the game by limiting the choice of props to a specific play theme. The paper plate would become something that could be used in a spaceship: an instrument dial, a steering wheel, or a round window. When playing this game, it is important for teachers to encourage children to use both gestures and words to describe how they are using the object in a pretend way. In some cases, teachers can place the objects used for the game in the play area so children can use them in the new ways in later play.

Helping children act out various roles

In mature play the set of roles associated with a theme is not limited and stereotypical but is easily expanded to include supporting characters. Playing hospital does not mean the only roles are those of doctor and patient. A nurse, lab technician, dietitian, and pharmacist can also participate. Patients can bring their parents or children with them; they can be brought by an ambulance driver or the pilot of an emergency helicopter.

Being able to choose among a variety of roles decreases the number of disagreements that are common when several children want to be the doctor and nobody wants to be the patient. In addition, when children get to play different roles in different scenarios, they learn about social interactions they might not have in real life (following commands and issuing them; asking for help and helping others; being an expert and being a beginner).

The ability of young children to act out various roles depends on their familiarity with what people do in different settings, how they interact with each other, what kinds of tools they use, and so on. Children are not likely to gain all this knowledge on their own. Teachers can help children expand the number of themes in their play and the number of roles associated with different play themes.

Field trips, literature, and videos are wonderful resources for expanding children's repertoire of play themes and roles. However, taking children on a field trip does not necessarily ensure that they will incorporate this new experience in their play scenarios. The most common mistake is to focus children's attention on the *things* part of a field trip or video—what is inside a fire truck or what happens to the letters when they arrive at the post office. Instead, teachers should point out the *people* part of each new setting—the many different roles people play in each setting and how the roles are related to each other.

Learning about new roles and the language and actions associated with each of them helps children reenact these new experiences in their play. For example, on a field trip to a historic train station, without the teacher's help, the children notice only the large engine. But with the teacher's help, they can learn about the roles of engineer, stoker, and conductor. They can talk about the passengers boarding the train, stowing their luggage on the overhead rack, and giving their tickets to the conductor.

This attention to the people aspect of the field trip will translate into more complex play back in the classroom. When the focus is on the objects, children's play may be limited by the number of appropriate props—imagine the difficulty of sharing one engineer's hat! However, when the focus shifts to the people and their roles, children can easily make up for the missing objects by substituting others or simply by naming them: Vincent says, "I am the engineer," as he pretends to put on his engineer's hat and then makes gestures as if he were holding on to a steering wheel.

Helping children plan their play

In mature play, children can describe to each other what the play scenario is, who is playing which role, and how the action will happen.

Teachers should point out the *people* part of each new setting—the many different roles people play in each setting and how the roles are related to each other.

Marcie says, "Let's pretend that I'm the teacher and these will be the students and you'll be a student. Then we'll read a book and sing our song together. Maggie [pointing to a toy bear] will be bad." "No, I want to be the teacher," says Jason. "OK, I'll read the book first, and then you'll be the teacher," says Marcie.

During this planning period, Marcie and Jason discuss how to handle the fact that both of them want to be the teacher.

© Ellen B. Sennisi

To get children to the point where they can do this mature planning, teachers have to encourage children to discuss

the roles—who they are going to be,

the theme of the play—what they are going to play, and

how the play will unfold—what is going to happen.

Teachers should set aside time to discuss this before the children enter the center. The children should focus on what will be played, who will be which person, and what will happen. At first the teachers will need to do some prompting, because children are used to discussing what they will play with or which center they will play in rather than the roles and themes of their play. Children who are going to the same center should discuss their plans with each other. We have found that children begin to use the discussion as a strategy for play itself. The planning helps children maintain and extend their roles.

Do play and foundational skills need to compete for the teacher's attention in an early childhood classroom?

Our research shows that an emphasis on play does not detract from academic learning but actually enables children to learn. In classrooms where children spent 50 to 60 minutes of a two-and-a-half-hour program in play supported by teachers' use of Vygotskian strategies to enhance play, the children scored higher in literacy skills than in control classrooms (Bodrova & Leong 2001).

Because children could play intensely during their center time, teachers had more time for meaningful one-on-one interactions with children. Group times were short and sweet because all the children were able to participate and pay attention. There was more productive time to learn, more time to be creative, and more time to have fun! Teachers commented that there was little fighting, a lot of discussion, and more friendships as children had many more positive interactions with each other than in previous years.

Mr. Drews decides to promote mature play in his classroom by following up on the Chinese New Year. He finds a book on Chinese restaurants, and he plans a field trip to a local Chinese restaurant. He asks May's parents to come to school to share the food that the family cooks and eats at home. He helps the children brainstorm the different restaurant roles—the cook, the person who seats you, the busboy, the customers. Children make their own food out of paper. They brainstorm the props that work best. Children's play really begins to improve. The restaurant play spreads from housekeeping to other play centers as children call in their orders to the restaurant by phone.

Play does not compete with foundational skills: through mature play, children learn the very foundational skills that will prepare them for the academic challenges that lie ahead.

References

Berk, L.E. 1994. Vygotsky's theory: The importance of make-believe play. *Young Children* 50 (1): 30–39.

Berk, L.E., & A. Winsler. 1995. *Scaffolding children's learning: Vygotsky and early childhood education.* Washington, DC: NAEYC.

Bodrova, E., & D.J. Leong. 1996. *Tools of the mind: The Vygotskian approach to early childhood education.* Englewood Cliffs, NJ: Merrill/Prentice Hall.

Bodrova, E., & D.J. Leong. 2001. *The Tools of the Mind project: A case study of implementing the Vygotskian approach in American early childhood and primary classrooms.* Geneva, Switzerland: International Bureau of Education, UNESCO.

Bodrova, E., & D.J. Leong. 2003. Learning and development of preschool children: The Vygotskian perspective. In *Vygotsky's educational theory in cultural context,* eds. A. Kozulin, B. Gindis, V. Ageyev, S. Miller, R. Pea, J.S. Brown, & C. Heath. New York: Cambridge University Press.

Bodrova, E., D.J. Leong, J.S. Norford, & D.E. Paynter. 2003. It only looks like child's play. *Journal of Staff Development* 24 (2): 47–51.

Bodrova, E., D.J. Leong, D.E. Paynter, & R. Hensen. 2002. *Scaffolding literacy development in a preschool classroom.* Aurora, CO: Mid-continent Research for Education and Learning.

Corsaro, W.A. 1988. Peer culture in the preschool. *Theory into Practice* 27 (1): 19–24.

Davidson, J.I.F. 1998. Language and play: Natural partners. In *Play from birth to twelve and beyond: Contexts, perspectives, and meanings,* eds. D.P. Fromberg & D. Bergen, 175–83. New York: Garland.

Elkonin, D. [1971] 1977. Toward the problem of stages in the mental development of the child. In *Soviet developmental psychology*, ed. M. Cole, 538–63. White Plains, NY: M.E. Sharpe.

Elkonin, D. 1978. *Psychologija igry* [The psychology of play]. Moscow: Pedagogika.

Fantuzzo, J., & C. McWayne. 2002. The relationship between peer-play interactions in the family context and dimensions of school readiness for low-income preschool children. *Journal of Educational Psychology* 94 (1): 79–87.

Howes, C., & C.C. Matheson. 1992. Sequences in the development of competent play with peers: Social and social pretend play. *Developmental Psychology* 28 (4): 961–74.

Krafft, K.C., & L.E. Berk. 1998. Private speech in two preschools: Significance of open-ended activities and make-believe play for verbal self-regulation. *Early Childhood Research Quarterly* 13 (4): 637–58.

Newman, L.S. 1990. Intentional and unintentional memory in young children: Remembering vs. playing. *Journal of Experimental Child Psychology* 50 (2): 243–58.

O'Reilly, A.W., & M.H. Bornstein. 1993. Caregiver-child interaction in play. *New Directions in Child Development* 59: 55–66.

Roskos, K., & J. Christie. 2001. Examining the play-literacy interface: A critical review and future directions. *Journal of Early Childhood Literacy* 1 (1): 59–89

Sigel, I. 2000. Educating the Young Thinker model from research to practice: A case study of program development, or the place of theory and research in the development of educational programs. In *Approaches to early childhood education*, 3d ed., eds. J.L. Roopnarine & J.E. Johnson, 315–40. Columbus, OH: Merrill/Macmillan.

Smilansky, S., & L. Shefatya. 1990. *Facilitating play: A medium for promoting cognitive, socio-emotional, and academic development in young children.* Gaithersburg, MD: Psychological and Educational Publications.

Vygotsky, L.S. [1966] 1977. Play and its role in the mental development of the child. In *Soviet developmental psychology*, ed. M. Cole, 76–99. White Plains, NY: M.E. Sharpe.

Vygotsky, L.S. [1930–35] 1978. *Mind in society: The development of higher psychological processes.* Cambridge, MA: Harvard University Press.

Who Owns the Subject?

Vivian Gussin Paley

During my visit to a child care center, the teacher makes it clear that she knows who owns the subject in the doll corner.

Marni, a three-year-old, has been rocking an empty crib for 10 minutes, humming to herself and glancing at a doll's arm visible under a pile of dress-ups.

"Where's the baby?" Mrs. Simon asks. "That crib is very empty."

"My baby went to someplace. Someone is crying." Marni stops rocking the crib and looks around. "Lamar, did you see my baby?" she asks a tall boy at the sand table.

"Yeah, she's in a dark forest," he says. "It's dangerous in there. You better let me go. It's down in this hole I'm making."

"Are you the daddy?" Marni asks. "Bring me my baby, Lamar. Oh, good for you, you finded her."

"Was she in a dark forest?" Mrs. Simon asks.

"Where was she, Lamar?" Marni says. "Don't tell me in a hole. No, not in a hole, my baby."

"Not in a hole, no. Under a tree under a bush under a mushroom under a big rock." Lamar is a year older than Marni and moves easily through the various options.

"I'll say where," Marni decides. "Under a big rock name Ginger-head. Ginger-head is the rock 'cause it looks like Ginger. That's my mommy, Lamar. Ginger."

"Good," Mrs. Simon agrees. "Safe and sound under a rock named Ginger-head. And now I see your baby is safe and sound in her crib."

"Safe and sound, safe and sound," Marni sings, placing a shawl over the doll.

The conversation between Marni and Lamar reminded me of one held by George and Emily in Thornton Wilder's *Our Town*. Seated at a soda fountain, with a sudden sense of intimacy, George says, "So I guess this is an important talk we've been having."

Vivian Gussin Paley writes and teaches about the world of young children. The vignette above is excerpted by permission from her book, *A Child's Work: The Importance of Fantasy Play* (University of Chicago Press, 2004).

The BUGS Are Coming!
Improvisation and Early Childhood Teaching

Carrie Lobman

In the toddler room Susan reads to children seated on the carpet. Several children eat dry cereal at the snack table. Two-and-a-half-year-old Mariel takes a huge handful of cereal and heads over to the block area.

"Mariel, you need to go back to the table to finish your cereal," Susan calls out.

Mariel pauses and points to the floor. "Bugs."

Susan looks down, then says to herself, *Whew! She's just playing. I told the children about crumbs attracting bugs months ago. Mariel still remembers. I can work with this.*

"Where are the bugs?" asks Susan.

Mariel points under the magnetic number board.

"Really?" Susan gasps in mock surprise, "Underneath the number board?"

Mariel grabs her friend Jessie's arm. "Jessie, bugs are coming." Jessie shrieks and begins running in circles. "The bugs are coming," the two girls chant in unison. The children listening to the story are now watching the action.

Uh oh, Susan thinks, *this is getting a little wild. But it's very interesting play. Maybe I should get involved.*

"You can see the bugs coming?" asks Susan. "Mariel, take a look at the floor. Is it clean?" Mariel nods excitedly.

"If you can see the bugs coming, I'd better make a call to tell them our floor is clean." Susan goes over to the telephone on the wall. "Hello, bugs? Don't come to our classroom; it's clean. OK?"

Susan hangs up. She announces in a loud voice, "The bugs won't come to our room. We keep our room cl . . ." She gasps and points at the floor. "Cereal?"

Carrie Lobman, EdD, is an assistant professor at the Graduate School of Education, Rutgers University, in New Brunswick, New Jersey. Carrie is an early childhood educator and an improv comedian. She was a founding member of the improv comedy troupe Laughing Matters, and she leads improvisation workshops for early childhood teachers and administrators.

Moments like this occur frequently in developmentally appropriate early childhood classrooms. When young children are free to explore their interests and make choices, they do and say unpredictable things. Teachers must continually choose how to respond, because at any given moment an activity can go off in an unexpected direction.

In this scenario Mariel responds to Susan's reminder about a classroom rule with the fantasy suggestion that there are bugs on the floor. For Susan, this response could be hilarious, annoying, cute, interesting, distracting, or frightening.

Should Susan act as an observer, allowing Mariel to play out her bug fantasy without joining in? Does she involve herself in Mariel's play in order to bring skills and information to the game? Is there a way to react that is not about deciding between these two options but rather is about responding to what is going on at that moment and creating something with the children?

Some might argue that Susan should be cautious about including herself in Mariel's bug fantasy. They would say that play is valuable for children because it belongs to them (Jones & Reynolds 1992). If Susan becomes involved, she might dominate the play and detract from the children's experience (Bennett, Wood, & Rogers 1996).

Others would encourage Susan to join the children's play, with the goal of introducing social skills and information about bugs and cleanliness (Kitson 1994; Wood & Attfield 1996). They could point to research showing that play is primarily useful to children as a learning activity (Meadows & Cashden 1988; Hutt et al. 1989; Smilansky 1990). From this perspective children's learning increases when teachers involve themselves as co-players.

Both perspectives have merit. Each encourages teachers to be thoughtful in their interactions with children. However, I believe that we teachers often miss opportunities for creative and meaningful interactions when we reduce the choice to one between child-centered activity and teacher-directed activity.

Improvisation and the early childhood classroom

Another way to view the interaction between Susan and the children is as an improvised scene similar to a performance on television or at a comedy club. Thinking of the activity as improvisation reveals the ways in which early childhood classrooms are not purely child centered or adult directed, but are an ongoing collaboration. Everyone, teachers and children alike, contributes to the creation of a new, emergent scene. What is interesting is how Susan and the children spontaneously and collectively create it.

Just as the activity in an early childhood classroom resembles an improvised scene, improvisation in many ways resembles the pretend play of early childhood (Sawyer 1997b). As with children's play, theatrical improvisation is created without a written script or plot. It is an art form in which no one, not even the participants, knows where the game, scene, or story will end up, because it is being created as it goes along. Improvisers are trained to create, direct, and act collectively, all within view of the audience.

In many ways improvisation is the most ordinary of activities. People are not given a script at birth and advised to memorize their lines before they participate in life. They improvise every day—when they smile at others on the street, when they choose what to eat for breakfast, and when they engage in conversations. For the most part people are not conscious of their improvisational activity and are unaware of their improvisational ability. They think improvisation belongs on stage and is the sole domain of skilled actors.

Early childhood teachers deal with the unexpected all the time—spilled juice, lost gerbils, or broken zippers can interrupt even the most well-planned day. When teachers engage in improvisational activity, as Susan did, it produces a classroom environment where children's creativity is supported and developed.

Characteristics of improvisation

The characteristics of interactions in early childhood classrooms are similar to those of improvised performances. The main characteristics are spontaneity, not ruling out ideas, giving offers, building on others' offers, and the group's creating the scene collectively.

Being spontaneous. Spontaneity is the primary characteristic of improvisation (Spolin 1963; Johnstone [1979] 1992; Halpern, Close, & Johnson 1994). Performers must stay in the moment and not tie themselves to a particular goal or direction. Improvisation forces people to break with preconceived ideas about what is supposed to

Casey Sills

© Robbi Borine

© BmPorter/Don Franklin

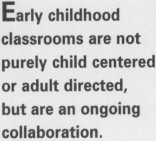

Early childhood classrooms are not purely child centered or adult directed, but are an ongoing collaboration.

happen and to go with the unexpected. Conscious spontaneity is not easy to achieve in a culture that values guaranteed outcomes and planned agendas. In this world, improvisational activity can feel unnatural.

Using everything. Improvisation depends on performers' willingness to use everything, including ideas they consider crazy, heretical, or just plain boring. It is based on a belief that people can create something worthwhile out of almost anything and that the unexpected is not a problem, but the seed of creativity. Improvisers create using whatever their fellow performers give them, even when it does not fit with what they wanted or anticipated. Improvisation is paradoxical—to be successful, performers must fully commit to their own suggestions and then be willing to go in a completely different direction.

Guidelines for Improvisers

- **Relate to yourself as a supporting actor.**
- **Do not enter a scene unless you are needed.**
- **Make your fellow actors look good.**
- **Trust your fellow players to support you.**
- **Do not judge what is going on except in terms of what you can do to help.**
- **Most of all, *listen*.**

(Halpern, Close, & Johnson 1994)

Giving and receiving offers. Improvisation is about giving and receiving offers (anything a performer says or does in a scene is an offer) (Halpern, Close, & Johnson 1994; Wacky World 2001). All offers must be accepted, and players must relate to everything that happens in a scene as real. For example, if two players are on stage and one says, "It sure is hot here on the moon," the other must accept that they are on the moon and build on it, adding something new. "Let's hike over to the dark side and see if we can find some shade" might be an appropriate response. Players trust that their fellow improvisers will be able to use their suggestions to create a successful scene.

Creating collectively. Finally, improvisation is about creating something collectively; one person is neither responsible for nor credited with the development of the performance (Spolin 1963; Halpern, Close, & Johnson 1994; Sawyer 1997a). The collective creation of the scene demands that the players work together, rather than focusing on individual ideas, goals, or egos. It assumes a commitment to the whole rather than the particular. The art of improvisation is the art of people creating collectively.

The improvised scene is extended

How is the interaction between Susan and the children improvisational? The scene began when Susan asked Mariel to take her food back to the table and Mariel responded playfully. There are several ways to interpret this exchange. From an improvisational perspective, Mariel's comment and Susan's response is the giving and receiving of an offer. When Mariel said "Bugs," Susan, in true improvisational fashion, accepted that the bugs were in the room and then went further by calling the bugs on the telephone. Throughout the interaction, Susan and the children picked up on each other's offers and then responded in ways that continued to develop the scene.

After Susan chose to accept and build on Mariel's offer of the bugs, the play continued.

> Susan hangs up the phone. "The bugs won't come to our room. We keep our room cl . . ." She gasps and points to the floor. "Cereal?"
> Mariel looks up at Susan and smiles. "Cereal!"
> Jessie leans down and picks up the cereal. Susan points with great urgency to the garbage can. "Hurry! Hurry! To the garbage, hurry!"
> Jessie runs over, drops the cereal in the garbage, and looks proudly at Susan.
> Susan pretends to wipe sweat from her forehead and breathe a sigh of relief. "Thanks, Jessie. All right, Mariel, I think we're safe. No bugs will come here."
> Mariel, sensing that the game might end, calls out, "The bugs!"
> Susan asks, "Where are they? In your lunch bag? Should I call them again?" Susan goes back to the phone, followed by four or five children who have come from the rug to join the play. "Hello, bugs, don't come here. We keep our room clean."
> Two-year-old Joseph points to a dirty spot on the floor and says, "I see bug."

First Sleepover

Gail Perry

Abby at age five was thrilled to be going on her first real sleepover, even if it was only to her cousin's house. She was dropped off in the late afternoon, so she and Colleen didn't have much time to play before dinner. After dinner Colleen's father read the girls a story and then announced it was time to go to sleep. Abby looked up at him and said in a quite determined voice, "I came to *play*, not to *sleep!*"

Gail Perry is the book editor for *Young Children*.

South Carolina Educational Television

© Kathy Sible

Susan listens intently on the telephone. "The bugs say there is some cereal on the floor and that's why they keep coming." She hangs up the phone. "Mariel, children, check the floor . . . check the rug . . . look everywhere."

Most of the 10 children in the group now crawl on the floor looking for bugs. Some take goggles and helmets from the dramatic play area and dress up as bug collectors. Others go into the bathroom chanting, "No bugs here, no, no, no." Several children sit around a toy telephone having a conversation with the bugs. The bug scene continues for 30 minutes.

In the middle of the scene, when much of the group had joined the play, one child stood at the light switch, turning the lights on and off (an activity he often did by himself). Susan looked over and said to him, "You're making sure the lights are on so we can see the bugs. Thanks, Takashi."

Susan was not the only one in the scene who picked up on offers. When Susan successfully included Takashi in the scene, Mariel ran over and searched for bugs on the floor where he stood. When Susan told the children the room needed to be checked for bugs, two children who had previously been on the periphery of the scene put on goggles and white protective hats and became bug collectors.

The children in Susan's class ranged in age from 20 to 35 months, and their language development was varied. Several, including Mariel, had well-developed vocabularies; others came from homes where English was not the primary language, and some were just beginning to use verbal language. This group would not typically be expected to sustain long periods of social or cooperative play. However, the bug scene lasted 30 minutes and ultimately included all the children. Children did not compete for control of the scene or for Susan's attention, because she suggested different ways for them to join in the play.

Teachers and children as improvisers

Viewing the classroom activity as an improvised scene shows the strengths of the teachers and children. From a theatrical perspective Susan served as a skilled improviser. She took a great deal of responsibility for the overall production of the scene, but she did not control the activity. She made sure that all the children could participate, listened for offers that might move the scene forward, and provided suggestions to help shape the scene. As an improviser, Susan looked out for the overall success of the scene and fully supported her fellow performers—in this case, the children.

If Susan is viewed as a skilled improviser, the children can be viewed as naturally gifted improvisers. Children improvise all the time, largely because they do not always know what is supposed to happen. Adults know that B follows A, and they have difficulty thinking that things could be otherwise.

One of the key elements of good improvisation is that its progression is nonlinear: there is never a single right or appropriate response to an offer. Good improvisers make offers that others do not expect. In the bug interaction, from the beginning the children provided many of the unexpected or unconventional offers. Their offers took the scene beyond a predictable conversation about classroom cleanliness. Skilled teachers can help

Children can be viewed as naturally gifted improvisers.

create an environment where children's offers are used to move classroom activities in new and interesting directions.

What does improvisation offer?

Spontaneity, unexpected events, and working with a group of people—what day in an early childhood classroom does not include these features? Furthermore, what early childhood teacher does not struggle to respond to these very things, sometimes viewing them as problems or obstacles to the goal of creating a developmentally appropriate learning environment for the children?

Improvisation requires people to break with preconceived ideas and make the most of unexpected events. It calls for a spirit of collaboration and the group's commitment to working collectively rather than following individual pursuits.

Improvisation provides a way of thinking about teaching that more accurately reflects the real world of the classroom. When teachers view classroom interactions as improvisations, not child-centered or teacher-directed activities, and see themselves and the children as improvisers, teachers can expand the potential for creative interactions. These interactions can foster an environment where children learn to make use of their creativity in ways that support the development of the group.

Improvisation Concepts

Spontaneity: Performers must stay in the moment and not become tied to a particular goal or direction.

Everything is useful: Improvisation depends on the performers' willingness to use everything.

Giving and receiving offers: *Offers* are anything a performer says or does in a scene. All offers must be accepted.

"Yes, and . . .": Improvisers build on offers by adding something new. Every time improvisers speak or move in a scene, they strive to build on what came before and add something that will take the scene further.

Creating collectively: One person is neither responsible for nor credited with the development of a performance.

References

Bennett, N., L. Wood, & S. Rogers. 1996. *Teaching through play: Teachers' thinking and classroom practice.* Philadelphia, PA: Open University.

Halpern, C., D. Close, & K. Johnson. 1994. *Truth in comedy: The manual of improvisation.* Colorado Springs: Meriwether.

Hutt, S., C. Tyler, C. Hutt, & H. Christopherson. 1989. *Play, exploration, and learning: A natural history of the preschool.* London: Routledge.

Johnstone, K. [1979] 1992. *Impro: Improvisation and the theater.* New York: Routledge.

Jones, E., & G. Reynolds. 1992. *The play's the thing: Teachers' roles in children's play.* New York: Teachers College Press.

Kitson, N. 1994. "Please, Miss Alexander, will you be the robber?" Fantasy play: A case for adult intervention. In *The excellence of play,* ed. J. Moyles, 88–98. Philadelphia, PA: Open University.

Meadows, S., & A. Cashden. 1988. *Helping children learn: Contributions to a cognitive curriculum.* London: David Fulton.

Sawyer, R.K. 1997a. Improvisational theater: An ethnotheory of conversational practice. In *Creativity in performance,* ed. R.K. Sawyer, 171–93. New York: Ablex.

Sawyer, R.K. 1997b. *Pretend play as improvisation: Conversation in the preschool classroom.* Hillsdale, NJ: Erlbaum.

Smilansky, S. 1990. Sociodramatic play: Its relevance to behavior and achievement in school. In *Children's play and learning,* eds. E. Klugman & S. Smilansky, 18–42. New York: Teachers College Press.

Spolin, V. 1963. *Improvisation for the theater.* Evanston, IL: Northwestern University.

Wacky world of improvisational comedy. 2001. Online: www.geocities.com/Hollywood/Land/8017

Wood, L., & J. Attfield. 1996. *Play, learning, and the early childhood curriculum.* London: Paul Chapman.

Everyone Can Play a Role

Cleta Booth

A large group of older children, kindergarten through fifth grade, are drawn to the prekindergarten room for the weekly mixed-age "integration" hour. They are attracted by our classroom's recently organized hospital, complete with operating room.

One patient lies on the table while three fifth-grade girls take charge, preparing to perform a heart transplant. Pre-K and kindergarten children staff the hospital kitchen, a pre-

K doctor cradles his stuffed tiger, listening carefully with his stethoscope, and third-grader Ellen, a child with Down syndrome who has been part of our school community since she was two, struggles into a scrub suit. Like the younger children, Ellen seems to be on the fringe, engaged in parallel play and perhaps unaware of the medical drama unfolding.

While the surgeons do an X-ray, attach an IV, monitor blood pressure and heart rate, administer anesthesia, and finally begin to work with their imaginary scalpels, Ellen pulls on shoe covers, hair cover, and rubber gloves. Then she wanders away

from the scene, turning her back, busy with some imaginary objects.

Just as the head surgeon pronounces the successful removal of the patient's defective heart, Ellen turns around. She walks directly to the operating table with great dignity, head up and hands cupped wide in front of her.

"Here's the new heart," she announces.

The surgeons accept it with the same seriousness and quickly complete their surgery on the rapidly recovering patient.

Cleta Booth is the prekindergarten teacher at the University of Wyoming Lab School. She has participated in international delegations on early childhood special education and on play in education. Cleta has published articles in *Young Children* on play and project work.

Making Sense of OUTDOOR Pretend Play

Jane P. Perry

Children need to be outside just to let off steam, right? Should we see outdoor play as a break from learning, or as part of our planned environment? From the children's perspective, whether adults recognize it or not, the play yard is most definitely part of their learning environment.

The play yard is the place where children go to make sense of their world, most often with playmates and by engaging in pretend play (Perry 2001). Recognizing that the play yard is part of our classroom is a first step in appreciating the powerful value of outdoor play (e.g., NAEYC 1998).

This article focuses on the independent, outdoor pretend play of preschool children.

Complex learning happens in the play yard

When indoor and outdoor learning centers are designed to do the bulk of the direct teaching, children's pretend play in those centers can support and foster the bulk of their learning. When children play without relying on the accomplished skills of an adult, they tackle complex challenges in language skills, perspective taking, representational thinking, problem solving, and turn taking as they work hard to keep their games going.

What are they learning outdoors that they could not learn inside? Outdoors, children use natural materials such as water, dirt, tanbark, sand, and leaves to follow their own inventiveness. The large spaces allow children to use the whole body to explore, plan, and carry out their plans without restrictions on noise or

> **T**he large spaces found outdoors allow children to use the whole body to explore, plan, and carry out their plans without restrictions on noise or activity.

activity. Here in the play yard, children make sense of everything from the physics of how water flows, balls roll, and bodies push, swing, and hoist, to the basic social skills for getting along with each other.

Indoors flows into the outdoors

My full-day, faculty/staff child care classroom is part of the university's child study center. I am one of four or five adults on duty at any given time with 24 three- and four-year-olds. Trained university students assist career teachers to maintain this ratio. The child study center is designed with 70 percent of the learning environment outdoors.

We go outdoors, rain or shine. Doors to the yard stay open so the children can flow in and out as they choose where to play. Although not all programs have such easy access to the outdoors, the setup for learning through play can be adapted to a variety of settings.

Jane P. Perry, PhD, is research coordinator and a teacher at the Harold E. Jones Child Study Center at the University of California in Berkeley. She also works with the California Early Childhood Mentor Program, which improves child care through mentorship, salary enhancement, career development, and leadership.

Photos © Lynn Bradley.

Typically two adults are stationed outside. During today's shift from 9 a.m. to 1 p.m.—except for a half-hour indoor circle time—I will encourage children to explore and experiment with the outside learning centers. Children can choose to play in any one of several centers: a play kitchen with sand and water; a table for drawing and writing; activity tables for art, cars and unit blocks, Duplos, and puzzles; a sandbox area; a climbing structure; ball or trike play; and a tire swing. I want children to find a place in which to get involved and to stay and play.

A learning center guides children's learning through play with its available materials, objects, and space; what children naturally enjoy doing with those materials; and the shared history of play in that area. I arrange each learning center to be inviting and accessible for children: toys and materials are tidy, ordered on uncluttered open shelves, and well stocked. The space is defined: a table has two chairs; a sandbox has two hills with two shovels on each hill; the climbing structure is a lion's den now, later it is a firehouse.

Teachers complement children's play

Each learning center is separate from other areas to promote focused activity. The teacher's role is to complement the children's desire to play and imagine together. Teachers watch and support how children

begin play, how they figure out what to do together, and how they then play together.

Why is it so important that children play outside? A climbing structure, sand area, and tire swing suggest physical challenges but leave the theme of play up to the children. As preschoolers begin to identify with each other as a group separate from the adults in their lives, they seek out their peers for friendship and feelings of control and accomplishment. These social skills, gained in the company of each other, are the predictors of academic achievement and school adjustment in the primary grades (Pellegrini & Blatchford 2002).

The importance of place

When the play yard has defined and protected places for small groups of children, these areas support children's complex thinking and communication. Once children have played "making noodles" in the sand kitchen, "hunting for foxes" in the wood chips, or "firefighters" with the big blocks, their recollection of that event becomes as concrete a cue for future play as the bowl and spoon, the rakes, or the fire hats offered on succeeding days to encourage small group imaginative play.

My job in supervising the play yard is to honor the history of children's play from the days before and to set up defined spots where children can take up the game again. Then I watch how children use the curricular areas.

Aziza and Meli: What complex outdoor play looks like

As a teacher, part of my role is to support the progression of children's play with each other, day after day, month after month. I notice Aziza and Meli, both three years old, in the sandbox. In my half of the yard, two other children huddle together over a table of bird finger puppets and tiny pumpkins. A threesome takes turns pushing each other on the tire swing. Two more children sit on large blocks, fire hats on, grasping the attached steering wheels and whooping out their alarm sirens. I grab a clipboard, paper, and pencil and

> **M**y job is to honor the history of children's play from the days before and to set up defined spots where children can take up the game.

position myself to see my supervision area. Then I begin writing.

Meli digs a hole in the sand. "I'm making it fat," she explains.

Thinking of our class bunny, Aziza adds, "Fat for Byron to lie in. Then he can lie in the hot sun and burn out his fur." She sprinkles sand into the hole.

"What's the dry sand for?" Meli asks.

"What we're putting in is called Big Ammilium," Aziza responds. "Say *Big.*"

"Big."

"*Ammilium.*"

"Amilia."

"Ammilium," Aziza corrects. "Big Ammilium. Spell it: A-L-A." Aziza reaches for a see-through plastic tube and places it in Meli's hole. "It's a trap, see? Caught. When it catches any bug, it snatches it and takes the blood away."

"You mean pretend orilium?" asks Meli.

"Aluminum," Aziza corrects again. She sifts sand into the upstanding plastic tube. "And this bug catcher is going to get trapped, and my mom says it's my turn for the hole."

"But I don't want your mom to say it's your turn, it will make me sad," says Meli.

Aziza looks at Meli.

Meli pulls the tube out of her hole. "Then I throw it away," and she tosses the tube.

"That's not good, Meli, because then the bugs have nowhere to go to get trapped," says Aziza.

"Pretend we share this, OK? " suggests Meli.

"Yeah, and the bugs get trapped."

After five minutes of frenetically keeping pace with Aziza and Meli, the observation period ends. Aziza and Meli have experimented with new language, word sounds, and letters; they have negotiated different perspectives, practiced taking turns and sharing, and experienced the complexity of thinking involved in switching from the real world to the world of imagination and back again.

Watching for the progress of play

Children's pretend play with each other follows a pattern: initiating play, negotiating what the game is going to be about, and then acting out the game.

Sample Outdoor Setting for Preschool and Primary Grades

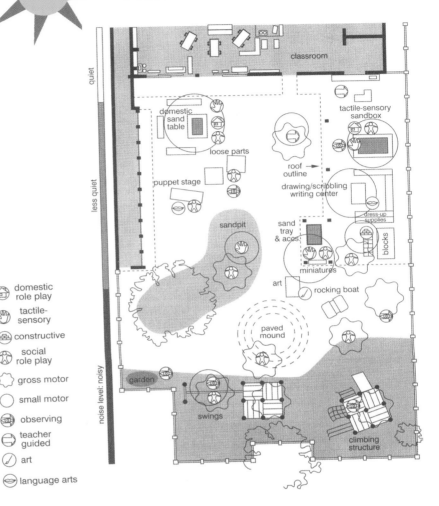

Play at the Center of the Curriculum, 3/E by Van Hoorn/Nourot/Scales/Alward, copyright © 2003. Reprinted by permission of Pearson Education, Inc., Upper Saddle River, NJ.

Initiation

During initiation, children are deciding with whom to play. This is relatively easy when children have had a lot of practice or when they have regular play partners—a special friend or two.

In other cases children new to play may desire companionship but have no idea how to begin. "No one wants to play with me" means a child is ready for practice. The tire swing is one sure bet in facilitating initiation, because it guarantees eye contact. Coaching children to use key phrases is another helpful strategy.

The tire swing is one sure bet in facilitating initiation, because it guarantees eye contact.

"There's Jaleel in the sand. Go over and say, 'Here I am.'" Direct contact can be overwhelming for some children, and simply setting up a play spot for side-by-side play is the first step on the road to independent play with another child.

Sometimes a child is so eager and attracted to the focused play of others that he or she will attempt to enter play by barging in and getting a rise from the others. The teacher can help by suggesting that the child first watch to see how the game works and then use language to enter the play, such as "Hey, guys, what are you doing?"

Often a child who is chasing another child wants to play but is misunderstood by others as meaning harm. A teacher's "I think she wants to play" can help children understand each other's perspective.

Negotiation

During the negotiation phase of pretend play, children decide on the theme of their game. Willie wants to play "good guy." He chases Ellie, pulling her arm to slow her down. I prompt a tearful Ellie: "Ask Willie. Say: 'How come you're pulling my arm?'" Willie is clear: "Because you are the bad guy, and I'm the good guy and I'm catching you." Willie is coached to ask Ellie first if she *wants* to be the bad guy. This is a revelation to Willie, who is learning how to negotiate what game he will play with others.

Sometimes a group's fast pace results in indiscriminate interruption of other play in the yard. "Hey, you three, what are you doing?" I ask to help them think out loud about the details of their game. Teachers can help children think up roles to act out in their games; for example, if they are playing kitties, I ask if they have a parent, siblings, or cousins. When children's imaginations need a nudge, the teacher can suggest a game observed in the past.

Enactment

In the enactment phase, children act out the game. I watch for disagreements that threaten to end the game, help identify player intentions when they are confusing, and model the use of language and play voice to cue progressive developments in the game's theme. As needed, I also refer to safety rules.

In a group with diverse cultural backgrounds, different behaviors or ways of speaking can mean different things. I may need to help children slow down the momentum of the game long enough so that players can check on intentions. Noticing what fantasy role or theme children are playing and talking to them in the pretend role greatly facilitates problem solving when differences arise. In some instances the teacher may decide to participate as a player in the play theme.

Advocating for outdoor play

The play yard is one place children can go to feel the power and consequences of their own initiative in the context of the peer group. The outdoors can accommodate higher levels and different kinds of noise than the indoors. There is more space for healthy, vigorous activity. The outdoors opens up the senses, and, when well designed, the outdoor play area offers a chance to experiment with challenge and cause and effect (e.g., Rivkin 2000). Children can figure out how to begin an interaction, how to have and verbalize a plan, and how to negotiate along the way.

One way to advocate for outdoor play is to map out your yard just as you would carefully map out learning centers inside the center. Where can domestic play happen in the yard? Where can children use drawing, scribbling, and writing to elaborate on their game? What areas offer the complexity of planned constructions with blocks, with sand and water, with balls and gravity? Where can children run and chase? Dangle and hang and hoist? You don't need a great deal of space. We all know how to ingeniously arrange indoor space for defined activities. Look at your yard in the same way.

When you have mapped out the yard, look at how each area is defined or protected so small groups of two to four children can engage with each other with reasonable success. Is there a chance for children to play next to each other and observe the ease of master players? Are there spots that offer a respite from the crowd and hubbub?

Set up the area with the children's past histories of play in mind. Watch for the play group's next step, offering language, a new play prop, or some imaginative flexibility to encourage inclusiveness. Assess the

A Fly on the Wall
Recording Nonjudgmental Observations

1. Have clipboards, paper, and pencils handy. Pick a time when children are focused and engaged in learning centers independent of your direct intervention.

2. Pick one child to follow, including his or her playmates. Follow the child's actions, including self-dialogue and conversations with others, recording only what you see that child and his or her playmates do and say.

3. Refrain from making judgments or including expectations for what the child *should* be doing. Record only what the child *is* doing: "Andrew fingers the dry sand" rather than "Andrew isn't playing with anyone."

4. Respond to children's questions about what you are doing with a simple "I'm just writing down how kids play so I don't forget."

5. Complete your observation in five to seven minutes. Later, take time during a break to add any details you didn't write down at the time.

children's use of the outdoor learning centers through regular observation such as the one of Aziza and Meli. Use the observations in staff meetings to follow each child's development, and keep that information in a portfolio to share with families.

By thinking about setup and knowing how to watch and interpret play, you can ensure that teachers and children experience the physical, social, and intellectual vigor of outdoor play.

References

NAEYC. 1998. Early years are learning years: The value of school recess and outdoor play. Online: www.naeyc.org/resources/eyly/1998/08.htm.

Pellegrini, A., & P. Blatchford. 2002. The development and educational significance of recess in schools. *Early Report* 29 (1). Online: www.education.umn.edu/ceed/publications/earlyreport/spring02.htm.

Perry, J.P. 2001. *Outdoor play: Teaching strategies with young children*. New York: Teachers College Press.

Rivkin, M.S. 2000. Outdoor experiences for young children. ERIC EDO-RC-00-7. Online: www.ael.org/page.htm?&pd=l&index=237.

Martha B. Bronson

Choosing Play Materials for Primary School Children (Ages 6–8)

Children in this age range benefit from a number of the types of materials that support and nourish development in earlier years, as well as additional, more complex play and learning materials. Materials that facilitate social understanding and cooperative interaction continue to be important and can be expanded to include concepts in social studies. Children are increasingly peer oriented during these years and are better able to consciously cooperate, negotiate with each other, and stick to simple rules in games. They are also more apt to form groups that exclude others as they learn to use and create rules and strategies for social acceptance and successful interaction. Antibias materials and those that promote responsibility, respect for others, and cooperation may help to reduce these tendencies.

Materials that support creative expression in art, music, and movement also continue to be important. Many children develop an interest in formal lessons in one or more of the arts during this period, and some schools offer beginning group or individual instruction. Opportunities for creative self-expression can nourish awareness, sensitivity, and confidence. They can also provide another area for skill development and achievement for children in the early school years, who are now more interested in products and outcomes and more aware of their own relative performance.

An increasing variety of materials are useful and important for promoting the development of literacy, mathematical and spatial understanding, mechanical understanding, concepts related to nature and science, critical thinking, and understanding of the "scientific method." Well-designed materials can also support the development of "process" skills, which help children learn how to learn. Process skills include multiple and hierarchical classification, measuring, graphing, sequencing, planning, monitoring and correcting performance, hypothesis generation and testing, and logical inference.

Providing children the opportunity to choose and carry out learning activities independently supports the development of persistence, effective self-direction, and intrinsic motivation. Providing a variety of materials for children's independent learning activities (alone or with peers) is one dimension of effectively responding to individual differences in the classroom. When children have available a variety of materials at different levels of challenge and in a variety of interest areas, they can participate in a curriculum that meets their individual needs.

Social and Fantasy Play Materials

Mirrors

same as for adult use

Dolls

washable, rubber/vinyl baby dolls (with culturally relevant features and skin tones) (for younger children—age six)

accessories (culturally relevant) for caretaking—feeding, diapering, and sleeping (for younger children—age six)

smaller people figures for use with blocks or construction materials (for fantasy scenes and models)

Role-play materials

materials for creating and practicing real-life activities—play money with correct denominations, book- and letter-creating materials

Puppets

puppets that represent familiar and fantasy figures for acting out stories (children can also create their own)

simple puppet theater—children can construct one (children can create props and scenery)

Stuffed toys/play animals

realistic rubber, wood, or vinyl animals to incorporate into scenes and models or that show characteristics of animals being studied (such as reptiles and dinosaurs)

Play scenes

small people/animal figures and supporting materials with which to construct fantasy scenes or models related to curriculum themes

Transportation toys

small, exact (metal) replicas preferred by children of this age range are not usually used in school settings, but more generic small models are useful

construction or workbench materials for children to use to make models of forms of transportation

Exploration and Mastery Play Materials

Construction materials

a large number of varied materials for detailed construction and for creating models (can use metal parts and tiny nuts and bolts)

Puzzles

three-dimensional puzzles

jigsaw puzzles (50 to 100 pieces)

Pattern-making materials

mosaic tiles, geometric puzzles

materials for creating permanent designs (art and craft materials)

Dressing, lacing, stringing materials

bead-stringing, braiding, weaving, spool-knitting, and sewing materials now used in arts and crafts

Specific skill-development materials

printing materials, typewriters, materials for making books

math manipulatives, fraction and geometric materials

measuring materials—balance scales, rulers, graded cups for liquids, etc.

science materials—prism, magnifying materials, stethoscope

natural materials to examine and classify

plants and animals to study and care for

computer programs for language arts, number, and concept development and for problem-solving activities

Games

simple card and board games

word games, reading and spelling games

guessing games

memory games (Concentration)

number and counting games (dominoes, Parcheesi)

beginning strategy games (checkers, Chinese checkers)

Books

books at a variety of difficulty levels for children to read

storybooks for reading aloud

poetry, rhymes, humorous books, adventure books, myths

books made by children

Music, Art, and Movement Play Materials

Art and craft materials

a large variety of crayons, markers, colored pencils, art chalks, and pastels (many colors)

paintbrushes of various sizes

a variety of paints, including watercolors

a variety of art papers for drawing, tracing, painting

regular scissors

pastes and glues (nontoxic)

collage materials

clay that hardens

tools (including pottery wheels)

more complex printing equipment

craft materials, such as simple looms, leather for sewing and braiding, papier-mâché, plaster of paris, small beads for jewelry making, etc.

a workbench with more tools and wood for projects (with careful supervision)

Musical instruments

real instruments, such as recorders (sometimes used for group lessons in school settings)

a wider range of instruments for children to explore (borrowed or brought in by parents or special guests)

Audiovisual materials

music for singing

music for movement, including dancing (folk dancing by age eight)

music, singing, rhymes, and stories for listening

audiovisual materials that children can use independently

Gross Motor Play Materials

Balls and sports equipment

youth- or standard-size balls and equipment for beginning team play (kickball, baseball, etc.)

materials for target activities (to practice skills)

Ride-on equipment

(children may be very interested in riding bicycles, but this is no longer included as a school activity)

Outdoor and gym equipment

complex climbing structures, such as those appropriate for age five (including ropes, ladders, hanging bars, rings)

Note: Although the four categories provide a useful classification, play materials can typically be used in more than one way and could be listed under more than one of the categories.

Excerpted from Martha B. Bronson, *The Right Stuff for Children Birth to 8: Selecting Play Materials to Support Development* (Washington, DC: NAEYC, 1995), 110–11, 120–21.

Elizabeth Jones

Playing to Get SMART

Ten very busy children are in the house area. The youngest three-year-olds are investigating dress-ups, going through the kitchen cupboards, talking on the phone. They are finding out what there is to do here, engaged in the exploration preliminary to focused play.

The older four-year-olds are involved in elaborate cooperative play. Beautifully dressed up, five children sit on chairs they have arranged as a car. Ashley tells the teacher, "We've come home, and now we're going to sleep." She spreads two blankets on the floor in front of the car, and they all lie down. Ashley puts her full shopping bag by the cupboard and pretends to yawn.

Ashley gently taps each sleeper with her long string of beads: "It's time to get up." They all do, picking up the blankets.

Vivian puts her blanket on the shelf and picks up two large blocks from the adjacent shelf. "OK," she announces, "we will make something like a TV or something." She and two helpers start building, while Ashley moves chairs into a semi-circle. "OK!" says Ramon. "The movie is starting, you guys." "It's a TV show," says Vivian.

Elizabeth Jones, PhD, is a member of the human development faculty at Pacific Oaks College in Pasadena, California, and codirector of its Distance Learning Program. She is coauthor with Gretchen Reynolds of *The Play's the Thing: Teachers' Roles in Children's Play* and *Master Players: Learning from Children at Play.*

Photos © Ellen B. Senisi.

Play is practice in choosing, doing, and problem solving.

When children play, they are thinking, innovating, negotiating, and taking risks. They create make-believe events and practice physical, social, and cognitive skills as they engage in these events as if they were real. Teachers support play by providing a variety of things to do, observing what unfolds, and staying nearby to help as needed and to acknowledge children's actions and words.

Schoolwork and play

Most traditional schoolwork is designed to teach standard rules and classification systems to young learners. *Closed,* right-answer tasks are what we all associate with our experiences of school. Play, in contrast, is *open;* it doesn't have preset rules (Jones & Reynolds 1992).

Children at play are constructing their own rules and learning at their own rates. As they test hypotheses and argue them with peers, they gain confidence in themselves as learners rather than becoming afraid to make mistakes. Children at play are learning to deal intelligently with the world. They are playing to get smart.

Smart is commonly defined as skills and knowledge of facts learned by rote and by directed practice. Today many schools experience pressure to provide teacher-directed instruction, cut out recess and the arts, and standardize curriculum and evaluation. In schools everywhere, even in Head Start, tests are being mandated to measure success in meeting learning objectives.

Success in our rapidly changing world depends on being able to think creatively and quickly.

Early childhood educators understand, however, that one-size-fits-all testing is an ineffective way to measure the understanding and competence of four- and five-year-olds. Rather, through their documentation based on observation and conversations carried on in the context of children's active learning, teachers take responsibility for assessing each child's growth toward developmental objectives.

Bombarded from all sides with what Piaget called "the American question"—How can we do it faster? How can we make children learn more, sooner? (Hall 1970)—we need to remember that facts acquired in isolation become easily forgotten trivia. Early childhood educators, focusing on the development of children's initiative, have chosen to think of *smart* as being skillful in curiosity and critical thinking. It is through play with materials and relationships, invention of classification systems, and solving problems in dialogue with others that young children develop the basic skills they will need to become effective contributors to the health of a changing world.

Living in a changing world

Success in our rapidly changing world depends on being able to think creatively and quickly. The modern world is full of the unexpected, as the global community brings strangers together and offers them many life choices. Decades ago anthropologist

Margaret Mead wrote that we are "rearing unknown children for an unknown world" (1970, 75). That's the kind of world we live in; it changes.

Some of the things we were taught as children aren't very useful by the time we're grown up. Some of the things we really need to know now are things no one had ever heard of when we were children, and so we have to learn about them for ourselves, if we can. To be able to learn for ourselves and, perhaps most important, to like learning new things, we need to be skilled players who enjoy encountering the unexpected.

The rate of change in our world is unlikely to slow down in the future. Social problem solving is a life skill everyone needs more and more, as we encounter people who are not like us. There are few isolated communities any more—places where change is slow, social control is based on separateness of language and culture, and obedience to tradition is the highest virtue. Historically, all over the world strangers have been regarded as enemies—people not like us.

In many languages the word for *people* was synonymous with *our people;* there was another word for everyone else. War and oppression could be justified against those others. In a rapidly shrinking world, these are not viable solutions to the problem of the stranger. Like children, adults need practiced ways to ask, "Will you play with me? What can we do together?"

Democracy, no matter how imperfectly it works, holds a vision of the potential in everyone. John Dewey had a clear vision of democracy as built on the insights and talents of all its members, building community through respect for diversity (Cuffaro 1995, 103). That's a particularly important vision in early childhood education. Each young child is filled with potential for intelligence and for caring relationships with others. We owe it to children and to society to cultivate children's potential by respecting their need to play, and to cultivate adult joy and creativity in inventing child-friendly play opportunities for children.

Teaching children the skills of play

Play is a mode of response to experiences that can and should be taught in early childhood education. We teach young children to play by providing them with space, time, and materials; offering them support in problem solving; presenting new problems for them to solve; paying attention to their spontaneous interests; and valuing their eagerness to learn about the world in which we all live together.

By providing culturally relevant materials, a teacher of kindergartners from Southeast Asian immigrant families encourages play and problem solving:

From [the] children's drawings, dictated stories, and chats with the children, I found out how important fishing was to the families. At the water table I added fishing poles, magnetic fish, rubber sea creatures, rocks, shells, and tin buckets. This became an engaging, important place to play. Unfortunately it only had room for three, and many more wanted to fish. So, from construction toys the children invented fishing poles—the long, deep-sea kind. On pillows, which functioned as the bank, they sat, fished, laughed, and joked for an extended period of time. (Evans 2001, 69)

By imaginatively entering play that is beginning to fall apart, this teacher successfully extends it:

Two children are beginning to squabble in the playhouse. The teacher knocks on an invisible

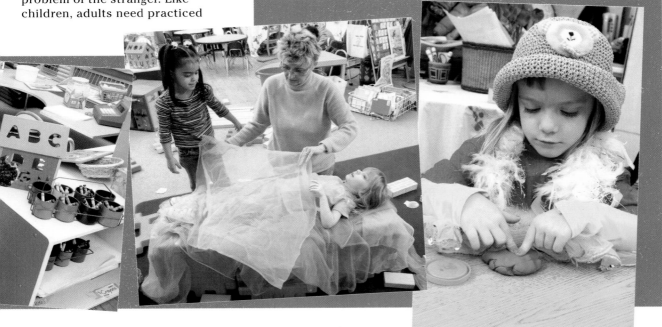

door. "May I come in? I've come to tea." The squabble stops, and they serve her graciously. "Is this Earl Grey tea?" she asks, sipping it. "No, it's soap tea," says one of the boys. (Reynolds & Jones 1997, 95)

By adding writing tools to the blocks and medical play equipment, this teacher extends the play to include literacy practice:

A group of children are building a hospital with large blocks, and playing with medical equipment to treat patients. The teacher puts a collection of signs, and tools for writing signs, on the adjacent table. Children quickly notice them and begin writing signs and taping them on the hospital. (Reynolds & Jones 1997, 95)

For school success in America today, early literacy has become the primary criterion. Often it is taught by rote. But standardized instruction ignores each child's relationship-based, meaningful experiences with language and literacy. In a literate society children pretend to be readers and writers just as they pretend to be shoppers and drivers of cars; they are spontaneously practicing adult roles to learn about them in ever increasing detail. Children playing together frequently correct each other, jointly shaping their understandings.

Within the safety of play, children sort out their current understandings and risk trying new possibilities. For example, four-year-old Erin is playing with pencil and paper and talking to her teacher Karen:

Erin writes E-R-I-H-H-D, and then moves her pencil across the letters several times, moving her lips as if she is reading.

Erin: Karen, I wrote bottle. Karen, I wrote bottle.

Karen: You wrote what?

Erin: Bottle.

Karen: [looking at Erin's paper] Bottle? Wow, look at that, Erin. You wrote bottle.

Erin continues to write more words and to read back what she has written. Later, she looks for the page where she had written bottle.

Erin: [softly to herself] Where's bottle? Where's bottle? [She finds where she had written E-R-I-H-H-D.] See? Bottle. Two-two-one-one-one-one. [while pointing to the letters E-R-I-H-H-D] (Owocki 1999, 97)

Erin is systematically constructing her knowledge of written language with spontaneous learning behavior reinforced by Karen's response.

Teaching adults the skills of play

Effective teachers of young children become skillful observers and co-players, not mere implementers of standardized curricula. Such a teacher leads group times based on her observations of play events, not on a preset plan. She can demonstrate the varied languages—speech and storytelling, drawing and writing—people use to represent and remember their experiences. Literacy is integrated into children's understanding as they discover, "My experiences make pictures and play and conversation," "My play makes stories," "My words make print." Teachers build bridges to literacy, as the following account illustrates:

Theresa likes to use her drawing skills as part of her own playfulness in teaching. One day she sketched the children at play, as one child was pretending to call the doctor on the phone and others were going for a ride on the "train" they had built of plastic crates. The next day she brought her drawing to circle time.

"Do you know what I saw yesterday?" she asked the children. "I saw Rosa talking to the doctor on the telephone. 'My baby is very sick,' she told the doctor. And I drew a picture of her. Do you see her?" Theresa held up the picture and the children squeezed close to see. "Rosa," they said. *Con el telefono.* Rosa, overwhelmed, put her hands over her face. Yolanda, who had been looking closely at the picture, burst out, "That's me! I driving!"

"Yes, that's Yolanda," agreed the teacher. "Yolanda and Juan and Diana and Alex and Joanie went on the train. And here they are."

"Our teacher drew our picture, and there we are!"

At the end of circle time there was a rush for the crates and chairs. Reminding children of their interesting play encourages them to repeat it, to understand and elaborate it more fully. (Jones & Reynolds 1992, 60–61)

In the scenario at the beginning of this article, Ashley, Ramon, and Vivian's teacher brings their story to circle time too, illustrating it with a few props from their play.

"Did you know," she asks the whole group, "that one, two, three, four, five children in our class built a car this morning? And that they got all dressed up and went for a drive? And then they all lay down and took a nap on this blanket? Ashley was wearing this long string of beads. Vivian was wearing these bright red shoes."

"I had on my cowboy boots," Ramon says in a big voice.

"So you did," replies the teacher. "Dwayne, what were you wearing?" Dwayne grins from under his hat brim. "A big hat! And you're still wearing it."

"I get mine, teacher," says Josué, reaching for the rack at the edge of the rug and pulling off an ID holder suspended from a cord. He puts it over his head. "See there? That's my name, right there."

"There are lots of ways to dress up," the teacher acknowledges. Then she holds up another familiar object. "Can you guess what this is?" she asks.

"It's just a block," say several of the children.

"Yes, it's just a block," agrees the teacher. "But sometimes children make blocks be other things. This morning it was a TV!"

Young children who are mastering play are endlessly imaginative. Teachers need to practice to keep up with them, and so it is important that teacher education and staff development include many opportunities for adults to create and critique curriculum ideas. Teachers need to play with materials—blocks, books, and paints—and with ideas and feelings, asking each other, "What else could you do with that? What could children do?"

Practice in telling stories and making up stories on the spot is essential. Teachers need to brainstorm curriculum possibilities: "What are all the different things people do at the store? How could you enrich that play with more ideas and props?" Play relies on *divergent* rather than *convergent* thinking; it asks, "What are all the ways . . . ?" rather than insisting, "This is the right way."

One child care center director invites her staff to brainstorm curriculum, webbing their ideas into a multidirectional action plan:

"'Collect shells' is something some of us liked to do as children and like to do as adults, too. Suppose you went to the beach this summer, and now you have a collection of seashells. . . . Suppose you've decided that the shells can be played with. What do you think are all the things that might happen, growing out of both your ideas and the children's? Let's see" . . .

A web is a *tentative* plan. It doesn't tell you exactly what will happen or in what order. That depends in large part on the children's responses. . . .

"So if I plan a unit on shells and it turns into dam building, that doesn't

mean I'm an awful teacher who keeps losing control?" asks Sandra.

"No, it means you're a teacher who's paying attention to children's interests, who's flexible and creative," says Bethany. (Jones & Nimmo 1994, 10–11)

Interpreting the meaning of play

The world today is full of good and bad choices among the many ways of constructing a life. Children, adolescents, and adults who are smart—skilled at play with things, ideas, and people—will have more capacity to create meaningful lives than people who are unable to tolerate ambiguity and the unexpected, who are stuck in defending the way things are or used to be.

Early childhood is the best time to practice these important skills and attitudes, because adults are there to keep things safe. And so, if you are a teacher of young children, think—playfully but thoroughly—about answers you can give to all those other people who criticize you by saying, "But the children are only playing. When do you teach them?"

References

Cuffaro, H.K. 1995. *Experimenting with the world: John Dewey and the early childhood classroom.* New York: Teachers College Press.

Evans, K. 2001. Holding on to many threads: Emergent literacy in a classroom of Iu Mien children. In *The lively kindergarten: Emergent curriculum in action,* E. Jones, K. Evans, & K. Rencken, 59–76. Washington, DC: NAEYC.

Hall, E. 1970. Jean Piaget and the American question: A conversation with Jean Piaget and Barbel Inhelder. *Psychology Today* 3: 25–56.

Jones, E., & J. Nimmo. 1994. *Emergent curriculum.* Washington, DC: NAEYC.

Jones, E., & G. Reynolds. 1992. *The play's the thing: Teachers' roles in children's play.* New York: Teachers College Press.

Mead, M. 1970. *Culture and commitment: A study of the generation gap.* Garden City, NY: Natural History Press/Doubleday.

Owocki, G. 1999. *Literacy through play.* Portsmouth, NH: Heinemann.

Reynolds, G., & E. Jones. 1997. *Master players: Learning from children at play.* New York: Teachers College Press.

Play

Children's Context for Development

Tovah P. Klein, Daniele Wirth, and Keri Linas

The four-year-olds are busy. "Go get some muffins, and we'll jump into the car," Sophie orders Nicholas. She and Issy run hand in hand to the slide. Underneath the slide their car awaits them—and their plan for a getaway.

Nicholas comes running back, his hands held out. "Here are the muffins," he says as he hands Sophie and Issy each a piece of warm, buttered air. "I'll drive," he says, skootching into the driver's seat.

Sophie and Issy wiggle backward to make room for their friend. Nicholas sits with his arms held out in front of him, gripping an invisible steering wheel. The girls wrap their legs around the person ahead, placing their hands on that child's shoulders—a three-child chain.

"Can I come with you?" yells Nina just before the car takes off. "Sure!" hollers Sophie. "Hop in back." Nina joins the chain, and with engine sounds they zoom away.

Tovah P. Klein, PhD, is director of the Barnard College Center for Toddler Development. She has been a preschool and child care teacher. Tovah's research focuses on parental influences on early socialization, and she is also studying the impact of 9/11 on young children and parents.

Daniele Wirth is a former assistant teacher at the Barnard College Center for Toddler Development. She is the founding director of the Learning Tree Child Care Center in Seneca Falls, New York.

Keri Linas, MA, is a research assistant and assistant teacher at the Barnard College Center for Toddler Development.

Photos courtesy of Tovah P. Klein.

Children's surroundings provide a world for exploration, discovery, and enjoyment. Playing is what young children spend most of their time doing from the moment they wake up until they close their eyes at night.

Grasping the significance of play helps us see inside the child's world and appreciate the impact playing has on development and learning. Through play, children learn about cultural norms and expectations, discover the workings of the world, and negotiate their way through their surroundings. Play teaches children about themselves, others, rules, consequences, and how things go together or come apart.

The importance of play is not accepted universally (Landreth 1993). Play is viewed by some as the opposite of work; play does not mean learning. Play is often trivialized in sayings like "That is mere child's play" or "He is only playing," as if to say play is unimportant. Many would prefer that young children spend their time tracing letters or matching figures on a worksheet.

This article defines the elements of play, illuminating its central role in young children's learning and development. The focus is on toddlers and preschoolers, age groups that spend most of their time involved in exploration and play (Fein 1981; Piaget [1962] 1999). Also addressed is the critical role of adults in supporting and extending children's play.

Characteristics of play

There is no universal definition of play. This is hardly surprising given that behaviors at one developmental stage can take on new meaning or functions at another stage (Howes 1992). Yet there are certain agreed-upon behavioral characteristics of play (Rubin, Fein, & Vandenberg 1983). The major defining characteristics of play are positive affect, active engagement, intrinsic motivation, freedom from external rules, attention to process rather than product, and nonliterality.

Positive affect refers to children's enjoyment of play as shown in their laughter, smiles, singing, and expressions of joy while playing (Schaefer 1993). Like adults, children seek enjoyable experiences and work to continue them; pleasure sustains the activity.

Two-year-olds Cecile and Peter stand facing each other in the sandbox, laughing. Cecile thrusts a shovel deep into the sand, then excitedly empties the shovelful of sand into the bucket between them. Peter laughs loudly as the sand pours into the bucket. He slides his shovel down into the sand, then hoists his own shovelful of sand into the bucket. The two spend a few moments laughing uproariously. They continue to alternate digging sand and dumping it into the bucket. Giggles abound.

Children's enjoyment of play is paired with another element, *active engagement*—deep involvement without distraction. Although this characteristic seems obvious, it is an important attribute; play fully absorbs children's interest.

Closely related to engagement and enjoyment is perhaps the most widely agreed-upon aspect of play—a child's *intrinsic,* or internal, *motivation* to play (Schaefer 1993). Different factors can motivate a child: novelty, gaining a new angle on a familiar experience, achieving mastery with known objects, needing to work through feelings. Although the motivation comes from the child, adults establish a safe environment and support or assist in the play.

Adults have an important role, but they do not make the rules for play. Instead, play occurs outside external rules as the rules and structure governing play come from the children (Landreth 1993).

Miguel stands by the doll cradle. He presses a doll wrapped in a blanket against his chest. Gabby tugs at Miguel's doll and snatches it from him. The teacher tells Miguel to "hold on tighter next time; it's really hard when you both want the same doll." The teacher offers another doll to Miguel.

The two children, both holding dolls, face each other. Miguel bows his head slightly and looks up at Gabby. Gabby, her face blank, abruptly drops the disputed doll. Miguel thrusts his doll toward Gabby. She reaches out with both arms and enfolds Miguel's offering in a hug. Miguel picks up the doll at his feet, holds it to his chest, and walks away smiling.

Teacher involvement decreases over time as experience helps children gain independence in negotiating.

The teacher's active support—defining the problem and offering an alternative—helped the children negotiate their own solution. Thus, no rule was imposed. With more verbal children, teachers can encourage each child to describe what is happening (that is, to define the problem) to guide them toward a resolution. Teacher involvement decreases over time as experience helps children gain independence in negotiating.

Freedom from external rules does not mean the total absence of rules. Children set rules governing roles, relationships, entry into play, plot development, and acceptable behaviors (Fein 1981). The players develop and agree upon the rules, which are implicitly understood.

It's cleanup time, and the pizza delivery girl makes an entry. "Who ordered a pepperoni pizza?" Texeira hollers as she carries a block toward the block shelf.

"I did," answers Ashook as he takes the block from Texeira and places it on the shelf. He is the block organizer, neatly stacking the wooden "pizzas" according to size.

Soon the other children begin delivering pizza. As they pass the blocks to Ashook, the chants echo through the classroom: "Who ordered a cheese pizza?" "Here's another pizza!"

> **The process is the activity; it keeps the children involved, exploring and discovering without a defined beginning or end.**

The children have distributed roles and created a structure for their pretend play to succeed. While the activity leads to a successful cleanup, the pretend aspects are what engage the children and sustain the play.

During play, young children *focus on the process* or performance of the activity, not on a goal or the results (Landreth 1993). It is this aspect in part that separates play from work. Here, the process is the activity; it keeps the children involved, exploring and discovering without a defined beginning or end. Players set the goals, and the goals can change in importance according to desire (Rubin, Fein, & Vandenberg 1983). The process allows play to take new directions and be transformed, curtailed, or extended spontaneously and without disruption to the activity.

Adults establish and guide the play environment. The environment serves to significantly facilitate the process of play.

Two-and-a-half-year-old Wally runs toward a large, floor-length Plexiglas mirror on the wall. As he reaches it, he leans forward with both arms raised high and slaps the mirror. Smiling at his reflection, he screeches. Still smiling, he turns around, flops into a pile of pillows, and laughs.

Watching him, Cameron joins in the laughter. She races to the mirror, slaps her hands against it, and makes a loud, high-pitched coo.

Wally sits up and turns toward Cameron. Cameron imitates Wally by falling onto the pillows. She shakes with unrestrained laughter.

It is unlikely that these toddlers began their play with a goal in mind. Their spontaneous movements

Facilitating and Supporting Children's Play:

Focus on the process (rather than the goal) of play. Ask exploratory questions that help extend the child's play.

- A child is making honking noises as he pushes a truck.
  Teacher: "Where is the truck going?" or "That is such a noisy truck. What is it honking at?"

- A child holds a baby doll in the kitchen play area.
  Teacher: "What does the baby like to eat?"

Elaborate and build on children's play or interests. Make comments, offer new and varied materials.

- A child is busy racing and crashing trains.
  Teacher: "Those trains really must be in a hurry. I wonder what they are doing."

- For children who enjoy the creative arts table (and to attract children who don't), offer varied art situations to support exploration, such as sponges, rollers, and different textures to paint on. This builds on children's interests while extending the types of experiences they have.

- Talk about what the children are doing or ask questions to support and extend their play.
  Teacher: "You are washing that baby. She must have been dirty," "I wonder where that pig is going now. Is he hungry?"

Reflect the emotions children express in their play and actions. This labels and validates children's feelings.

- A child stomps away from a peer who is using her favorite truck.
  Teacher: "It made you really angry when Jacob took your dump truck."

- A child sits quietly in a corner soon after her parent has left. Her head is down, and she is not engaged.
  Teacher: "You really miss your mommy. She always comes back to get you. It's OK to miss your mommy when you're at school."

Suggestions for Teachers

Define the problem. Help children learn negotiation skills. Encourage them to think about alternatives.

• Two children are tugging on a ball.

Teacher: "It looks like you both want that ball. What can you do to work this out?" If the children are too young or lack the verbal abilities to verbalize a solution, the teacher can try to define the conflict and offer an alternative: "It looks like you both want that ball. Here is another one just like it that one of you can use."

• One child grabs a marker away from another child, who then cries.

Teacher: "It looks like there is a problem here. Can each of you say what just happened?" If children are young and lack verbal abilities, the teacher can say, "It looks like you both need that marker. Next time, you can tell Lupe, 'That's mine!'" At the same time, she offers another marker.

• All of the desired toys are being used in the context of a pretend play situation. If a child looks around for a toy to use but is not engaged, suggest alternatives.

Teacher: "This rolling pin can be a pretend phone" or "This scarf would make a warm blanket."

Provide varied materials to encourage exploration and play.

• Provide materials not usually found at home—finger paints, a variety of musical instruments, dress-up clothes, hammer toys. These allow children to engage in open-ended and exploratory play.

• Supply natural and synthetic materials—feathers, leaves, sand, water, shaving cream (in the water table), Styrofoam, scarves, stickers. These provide a range of opportunities for exploration and play.

• Add "real life" toys, like kitchen utensils, blankets and pillows, and medical kits, that provide opportunities for symbolic play and to work out fears.

Provide open-ended materials for play.

• Wooden blocks, Legos and other building toys, and playdough all provide children with open-ended stimuli that allow them to play as they choose.

• Add props to encourage pretend play—people or animal figures in the block area, baby dolls or plastic dishes in the water table.

and emotions come from their enjoyment of the activity. The interaction develops as their excitement and shared pleasure builds, spurred by the enticing objects and the layout of the room. The teacher has established a play area with safe, developmentally appropriate materials (shatterproof mirror, pile of pillows) where children can play with minimal adult intervention.

This vignette shows the children's ability to cooperate and develop an imitative game without verbal communication. They communicate through their actions—running, laughing, falling down—and through imitation. Howes (1992) identifies the central social task of two- to three-year-olds as mastering the communication of meaning, or improvisation.

By this age, children can agree that "this is play" and distinguish between reality and play, allowing them to create games and shared meaning. Early play involves run-and-chase type games, which also require communication (Who runs? Who chases? When do the roles switch?), often nonverbal. As language develops, verbal negotiation is incorporated into the games.

The play-versus-reality distinction inherent in fantasy or pretend is called *nonliterality* (Singer & Singer 1990; Howes 1992). The make-believe world is a place where children escape reality, forgo limits, and have power over what they do (Singer & Singer 1990). By age two, as children become increasingly social, much of their play incorporates fantasy (Fein 1981; Howes 1992).

> **The play-versus-reality distinction inherent in fantasy or pretend is called *nonliterality*.**

> Lissa grabs a blob of blue playdough. She sticks tongue depressors upright in the playdough and holds the concoction out toward her friend. With a wide smile she sings, "Happy birthday to me . . ."
> The teacher comments, "It's your birthday. Will you have a party?"
> Lissa grins, puts her hands on her head, and says, "Here's my party hat!"

For the moment it is Lissa's birthday. The teacher builds on Lissa's fantasy ("It's your birthday. Will you have a party?"), guiding her to extend her play.

Exploring—gaining information about an object—is a foundation that often leads to playing. In exploration children ask, "What is this? What can it do?" The inquiry process enables discovery, familiarization, and feelings of competence and security ("This is something that I know"). By asking open-ended questions ("What does that feel like? What can you do with it?"), adults invite an unengaged child to participate and to expand the involvement of those already engaged (Tegano, Sawyers, & Moran 1989).

How does play support learning and development?

Enrichment and growth naturally evolve from playing as children learn about themselves and their surroundings. A child's active participation in his or her world facilitates mastery and control, leading to feelings of competence and self-efficacy. Both contribute to young children's sense of self (Pruett 1999). The internal excitement derived from discovery and mastery nurtures children's innate desire to learn. This passion and internalized sense of accomplishment is what motivates children's learning.

Play lets children make important discoveries about the self—including their own likes and dislikes. They continually shift activities to maximize pleasure, while discovering what is easy and hard to do and what makes them happy or frustrated. They learn to understand the feelings of others and develop empathy. These skills are crucial for healthy peer relationships.

Julia, nearly three, cries at her mother's departure. "It's OK to cry when you're sad," the teacher quietly reassures the child slumped in her lap. "Mommies and daddies come back."

Harry, perched on a chair nearby, closely watches the scene. He wiggles off the chair, slowly approaches Julia, and hands her a teddy bear. Harry repeats the teacher's mantra: "Mama come back soon."

Play fosters language skills. Pretend play encourages language development as children negotiate roles, set up a structure, and interact in their respective roles (Garvey [1977] 1990). Adults support language by commenting on or labeling children's play ("I see you are washing that baby," "That's a big blue painting you're making!"). Such comments provide a language-rich environment and naturally reinforce concepts and build on the play.

The internal excitement derived from discovery and mastery nurtures children's innate desire to learn.

Language is tied to emotions, which are expressed and explored through pretend play (Slade 1994). Pretending gives children the freedom to address feelings, anxieties, and fears. Through fantasy, children re-create and modify experiences to their liking. They foster a sense of comprehension, control, and mastery (Schaefer 1993). This can enhance feelings of security.

The peekaboo or run-and-chase games played by older infants and toddlers are a rehearsal of the going away and coming back of the parent, at the child's determined pace. As the adult exclaims "I came back" or "I caught you," the return is reinforced, providing a much needed message for children working through separation (First 1994).

"Grrrr, grrrrr." From the doorway between the cubby room and the classroom, a dry, raspy growl is heard. "Grrrrr, grrrrrr."

Three-year-old Sharie steps into the classroom, followed by her mother. Sharie's stance is tense and wide, braced for action. Her arms are outstretched. Her hands and fingers are scrunched up as claws. With teeth bared, Sharie gives another growling greeting to the teacher while clawing the air. Approaching the teacher, she stomps down hard with each step.

Sharie continues to growl and flex her claws. Then she turns to the mirror and growls at her image.

Becoming a ferocious lion allows Sharie to put aside the timid child who fears leaving her mother. Instead, being a fierce animal lets her test the waters and helps her cross into the classroom with confidence. The teacher can encourage or welcome the lion into the forest, noting the scary growl and offering materials like blankets to make a lion's den. In time, the lion will disappear and Sharie will enter the classroom as herself.

Four-year-old Ray is afraid of monsters and refuses to go to sleep at night. At school one day, he and his friend Mario put on police hats and carry bright orange foam bats—their "monster zappers." They follow the monster's trail, crouching low and giggling together. As they round a corner, they pounce on the monster and capture it.

"We got him now!" exclaims Ray, high-fiving his friend. The boys lock the monster in a box and throw away the key.

"You locked up the monster! He can't scare you anymore," notes the teacher.

In the safe confines of friendship, Ray is the conqueror rather than the conquered. His scary feelings and anxiety can be mastered in a contained and non-threatening setting. The teacher states the feelings Ray is working to master, which helps him better understand his emotions.

Pretend scenarios grow in complexity as children's symbolic capacities increase. This growth leads to more varied and elaborate scenes—as mother, father, monster, helicopter pilot—requiring children to negotiate roles and rules (Garvey [1977] 1990). Children gain

Superman

Mimi Brodsky Chenfeld

Red cape fastened to his back, he runs excitedly into my movement session with his class.

"Hi, Jackie," I call.

"I'm NOT Jackie, I'm Superman!"

While his classmates skip, leap, and hop around the room, Superman flies.

Each week, red cape floating behind him, he soars through our stories, poems, and songs. No matter what our curriculum, he is saving people and fighting evil. My challenge is to include Superman in EVERY session. And we do! For example, Superman flies with our Jack Be Nimbles, with Dorothy and her friends on the Yellow Brick Road, with Olympic athletes, and with migrating birds.

One day, SURPRISE! Jackie's class bounds into my room for its weekly session. Jackie is NOT wearing his red cape!

"Hi, Superman," I greet him.

He whispers to me, "I'm not Superman."

"OH, who are you?"

"I'm Clark!"

Lesson: Never underestimate the attention span of children totally involved in imaginative play! When children are fascinated by an idea they go on and on and on and on . . .

Mimi Brodsky Chenfeld, MA, is now in her forty-seventh year in education. Among her books are *Teaching in the Key of Life* (NAEYC), *Teaching by Heart* (Redleaf), and *Creative Experiences for Young Children,* third edition (Heinemann). She has traveled to 44 states carrying her message of joyful, arts-rich education for *all* our children.

more sophisticated communication skills and learn about social rules as natural outcomes of their play.

Adults can continue to reinforce and extend the play to sustain children's interest, or they can enter the play directly if invited. Labeling feelings and reflecting on emotional content is an effective way to extend fantasy play: "That lion sounds so angry." It can help children understand feelings by saying, "Why do you think that monster is so sad?"

Play is a vehicle for expressing feelings, with minimal language needed. Moving feelings from the child to the pretend character reduces anxiety and frees the child to explore emotions. The adult's message is "It is safe to have and express these feelings."

Adults also can reinforce actions: "That daddy is carrying a lot of groceries from the store. I wonder what he will do with them." This allows the child to think about the next step in the play sequence (Should the daddy cook? Where will he take the food?).

Play teaches children about the social world. It provides opportunities to rehearse social skills and learn about acceptable peer behavior firsthand. With age and experience, children's awareness of peers playing around them increases. This leads to more interactions between children and incorporation of peers into their play (Parten 1932). Group play provides a stage for rehearsing peer skills and learning to be a community member.

Both social and solitary play provide opportunities for children to practice problem solving and negotiating—skills needed to achieve competency in learning, in social relationships, and in being a group member.

Children who know the excitement of seeking out new information and finding things out for themselves also love to learn.

Conclusion

A child's world is filled with the magic of exploration, discovery, make-believe, and play—vehicles for development. Much of children's early learning comes through self-discovery—an outcome of play. We have defined and illustrated the elements of play as a way to better understand its essential parts, the development it fosters, and the adult's crucial role as a supporter of the play process.

Play is young children's most familiar and comfortable tool for engaging the world, with adults as essential scaffolds. Using observation and intervention aligned to children's developmental capabilities, adults provide a bridge from children's current to their future language, cognitive, social, and emotional processes.

Adult roles vary from commenting on play, extending the activity, and actively participating, to providing verbal interpretations, emotional support, and suggestions or alternatives. By setting up a supportive and inviting environment, adults let children take initiative, explore, play, learn, and experience the thrill of discovery. This is a critical link between play and more formal learning—children who know the excitement of seeking out new information and finding things out for themselves also love to learn (Pruett 1999).

For children, play is a dialogue with their surroundings—indoors or out, pretending or exploring, talking or being quiet, alone or with others. The rich complexities and subtleties offered through play provide a base for ongoing development. Not all children have opportunities to play in safe environments, but certainly all children deserve the chance to do so.

References

Fein, G. 1981. Pretend play in childhood: An integrative review. *Child Development* 52: 1095–1118.

First, E. 1994. The leaving game: The emergence of dramatic role play in two-year-olds. In *Children at play: Clinical and developmental approaches to meaning and representation,* eds. A. Slade & D.P. Wolf, 111–32. New York: Oxford University Press.

Garvey, C. [1977] 1990. *Play.* The Developing Child Series. Cambridge, MA: Harvard University Press.

Howes, C. 1992. *The collaborative construction of pretend: Social pretend play functions.* Albany: State University of New York Press.

Landreth, G.L. 1993. Self-expressive communication. In *The therapeutic power of play,* ed. C.E. Schaefer, 41–63. Northvale, NJ: Jason Aronson.

Parten, M.B. 1932. Social participation among preschool children. *Journal of Abnormal and Social Psychology* 27: 243–69.

Piaget, J. [1962] 1999. *Play, dreams, and imitation in childhood.* New York: Routledge.

Pruett, K.D. 1999. *Me, myself, and I: How children build their sense of self.* New York: Goddard.

Rubin, K.H., G.G. Fein, & B. Vandenberg. 1983. Play. In *Socialization, personality, and social development,* ed. E.M. Hetherington, 693–774. Vol. 4 of *Handbook of child psychology,* 4th ed., ed. P.H. Mussen. New York: Wiley.

Schaefer, C.E. 1993. *The therapeutic powers of play.* Northvale, NJ: Jason Aronson.

Singer, D.G., & J.L. Singer. 1990. *The house of make-believe: Children's play and the developing imagination.* Cambridge, MA: Harvard University Press.

Slade, A. 1994. Making meaning and making believe: Their role in the clinical process. In *Children at play: Clinical and developmental approaches to meaning and representation,* eds. A. Slade & D.P. Wolf, 81–110. New York: Oxford University Press.

Tegano, D.W., J.K. Sawyers, & J.D. Moran. 1989. Problem finding and solving in play: The role of the teacher. *Childhood Education* 66 (2): 92–97.

Where Did Your Idea Come From?

Cleta Booth

Three boys, ages four and five, make constructions with cardboard boxes and the tubes from toilet paper and paper towel rolls during free choice time. Suddenly the boys begin running through the classroom with their constructions, making "ssshhhhh" noises and announcing that they are "spraying people with smelly stuff—if you breathe it, you die." One child who is "sprayed" starts to cry.

When I ask the boys about their play, they repeat exactly what they have been saying. I ask them how they got the idea for a machine that sprays smelly stuff. One of the boys says, "We just thought it up." I ask if they have seen or heard about machines like that, but they say no.

Our classroom rule is that the children can build whatever they want for the purpose of taking it home, but they can't play guns at school. I explain to the children that this rule applies to their machines because the machines kill people and because other children don't like being shot or sprayed.

The boys' play takes place two days after I held a meeting with families to discuss how we might handle children's fears and responses to impending war, so I put a brief description of the play in the weekly family newsletter. I wonder whether the boys are acting out ideas about biochemical warfare, or if I'm reading too much into this.

Cleta Booth is the prekindergarten teacher at the University of Wyoming Lab School. She has participated in international delegations on early childhood special education and on play in education. Cleta has published articles in *Young Children* on play and project work.

Play, Policy, and Practice Interest Forum

NAEYC's Interest Forums address the diverse issues encountered in the early childhood education field. They provide NAEYC members with networking opportunities and the chance to participate in communities committed to learning and growing together. Interest Forums meet in conjunction with NAEYC-sponsored conferences and host Listservs that are free and open to any NAEYC member. To participate in forum discussions, visit NAEYC's Web site www.naeyc.org and click on Members Only.

The mission statement of the Play, Policy, and Practice (PPP) Interest Forum describes the group's purpose:

• to connect persons who share an interest in play,

• to update and disseminate current knowledge about the multifaceted nature and developmental value of play, and

• to become a collective voice within the early childhood community, advocating for the value and importance of children's play.

This forum's newsletter, *Play, Policy, and Practice Connections,* has been in continuous publication since 1995. Each issue develops a theme, and a guest editor invites teachers, researchers, and others to submit short articles expressing their ideas. Themes range from multicultural perspectives and building communities for play to the issue of standards and play.

To learn more about membership in the Play, Policy, and Practice Interest Forum, contact Sandra Waite-Stupiansky at SWAITE @edinboro.edu or Lynn Cohen at lynncohen@aol.com.

Thanks for the Memory
The Lasting Value of True Play

David Elkind

Last fall a parent observing at the Children's School at Tufts University complained about the amount of time the children spent playing. She told me that her friend's four-year-old son was in a program in which he was already learning his letters and numbers.

Mentally I rehearsed my usual spiel about the educational value of play and how much children learn from it. But it was shortly after 9/11, and I couldn't get myself to go through a litany of the academic benefits of play. Instead I surprised myself and said, "You know, they are having fun and enjoying themselves here and now, and this is every bit as important and valuable as preparing for the future."

I am not sure I convinced this mother, who was concerned that her own son might not be prepared for first grade. But I do think my response made her reflect a moment on her values and priorities.

Then and there I decided I would no longer advocate for free play on the basis of its intellectual, social, or emotional benefits. But I also began to ruminate on how best to justify letting children play for the fun of it. I first recalled Freud's response when asked what was necessary to lead a happy and productive life. He replied, "*Lieben und arbeiten*" (loving and working). With all due respect to Freud, I believe he should have added a third activity, namely, *spielen* (playing).

I believe that play is as fundamental a human disposition as loving and working. We play because we are programmed to play; it is part of human nature, and of animal nature as well. My family dog Remy patiently waits till we finish our dinner before he trots over with

> **I believe that play is as fundamental a human disposition as loving and working.**

a pull toy in his mouth to play a game of tug-of-war. It is his time to play, and he has no other purpose in mind than to enjoy the activity. In the same way children play because they are predisposed to play, not because they are trying to learn or achieve something. The truth is, children can't help playing.

Nonetheless, numerous theorists have expounded elaborately on the meaning and value of children's play. Their propositions have a measure of truth, but they look at play from the adult-functional rather than from the child-experiential point of view. Accordingly, in this article I present the value of play from the child-experiential perspective. First, I briefly review some more well-known and accepted theories of children's play, along with their limitations

Theories of children's play

The theorists discussed below seem to agree that play is important for the healthy growth and development of the young. They differ, however, in how they conceptualize the benefits of play.

Psychologist/philosopher Herbert Spencer [1820–1903] proposed that play was the result of advancing civilization. The higher the level of civilization, the less energy one must expend to obtain food, clothing, shelter, and protection. Our bodies have not changed, however, in accord with social progress. We remain programmed for expending large amounts of energy to ensure survival. Play is the means by which we discharge the surplus energy we once needed to meet our basic needs (Spencer [1896]1955).

In Spencer's view, children too have a great deal of surplus energy that they discharge through play. This theory, however, begs the question. After all, children

David Elkind, PhD, is a professor in and the chair of the Department of Child Development at Tufts University in Medford, Massachusetts. He is a former president of NAEYC and is best known perhaps for his books *The Hurried Child, Miseducation,* and *Reinventing Childhood.*

and adults can discharge excess energy in ways other than through play. Thus the question remains as to why people choose to discharge surplus energy by means of play rather than by walking, running, or other forms of exercise.

Zoologist Karl Groos [1861–1946] first studied play in animals and then looked at play in humans. He elaborated a thesis that the play of young animals was a form of preparation for their adult life (Groos 1898). He described the young kitten pouncing on a ball of cotton thread as practicing the skills it would need as an adult to catch its prey. Groos extended this concept to children's play as well (1901). When children engage in dramatic play, mimicking adult roles, they are preparing to carry out similar roles when they are grown.

One can hardly take this theory literally. I recently observed a young boy at an open-air restaurant put a napkin over his arm and proceed to take his parents' dinner orders. I do not really believe he was practicing for his future career. Is it necessary to read anything into this behavior other than that the child is having fun imitating adults?

One of the many people influenced by Groos was **Italian educator Maria Montessori [1870–1952].** She developed her methods and theory while working in Rome with children of families with few advantages. Perhaps because she felt the need to teach the children how to use tools, and because she developed her program during the straight-laced Victorian era, she was somewhat dismissive of free play and the use of imagination ([1912] 1964).

If children can fantasize fairy tale kingdoms, might they not put their imaginations to better use imagining foreign countries like America, Montessori suggested. Perhaps this is why she found the Groos work so attractive. It was Montessori who translated Groos's theory into the popular formula, Play is the child's work. Yet this is a false identification. Children work when they are learning to eat with a spoon or to hold a knife and fork. They play when they create their own utensils out of wood or clay. Montessori's dictum about play being the child's work and many of her didactic learning materials provided the rationale for the oxymoron *educational toys*. When grown-ups, with the purpose of teaching the child something, design a toy or a game, a child engaged with that toy or game is no longer playing in the true sense. We deceive ourselves, or ease our conscience, by referring to children interacting with these materials as *playing*.

Under the smoke screen of educational toys, a lot of academic material has been foisted on early childhood educators and young children. Children are at work when they are learning skills, knowledge, and values, whatever the materials are called. What makes children's play truly *play* is that it has no other aim than the pleasure of the activity itself. This is not to say that true play may not help children learn knowledge, skills, and values, only that true play is not engaged in for this purpose nor experienced as an accommodation to environmental demands.

> **U**nder the smoke screen of educational toys, a lot of academic material has been foisted on early childhood educators and young children.

Psychoanalyst Sigmund Freud [1856–1939] offered another explanation for children's play. In his classic book on dreams, Freud suggested that play, like the dream, was wish fulfillment (Brill 1938). Through dreaming and through playing, we are able to express socially unacceptable feelings, wishes, and desires. From this perspective, a child banging a doll against the floor might be getting rid of his or her aggressions against both parents and siblings. The doll is a substitute for the parents and siblings, who are all condensed within it and symbolized by it. And sometimes a child hitting a doll against the floor is simply a child banging a doll against the floor, and having a good time in the process.

This is not to deny that children sometimes use toys as therapy. When they do so, however, what they are doing is no longer play. In the same way, when we as adults attempt to discharge our anger and hostility through play, like slamming tennis balls, it is not really play because our actions have a deliberate goal. True play does not.

One of the broadest theories of children's play was proposed by **psychologist Jean Piaget [1896–1980].** Piaget was first and foremost concerned with the development of intelligence, adaptive thinking, and action. He proposed that intelligence progresses in a series of stages related to age and develops through the combined operation of two invariant processes, assimilation and accommodation. Through assimilation we transform the environment to meet the demands of the self. By contrast, in accommodation we transform ourselves to meet the demands of the environment.

> **S**ometimes a child hitting a doll against the floor is simply a child banging a doll against the floor, and having a good time in the process.

© Ellen B. Senisi

In Piaget's theory both play (assimilation) and work (accommodation) give evidence of the child's developing intellectual abilities (1951). The infant plays by transforming every object she touches into an object to be sucked. In this way the infant demonstrates a form of sensory-motor intelligence. During early childhood, the child acquires the ability to both learn and create symbols. The toddler demonstrates this ability both by learning language (accommodation/work) and by

creating new symbols (assimilation/play). The child who learns to say "Mama" and "Papa" appropriately gives evidence of the ability to learn conventional symbols. In the same way a child who holds up a potato chip and says, "Look, Mommy, a butterfly!" is demonstrating her ability to create symbols.

Although there is no question that the child is demonstrating new symbolic skills when he or she creates a new symbol, it is certainly not the child's intention to do so. The child is simply creating something and having fun doing it. Play does involve a transformation of reality, but this need not be purely in the service of intellectual growth.

Russian psychologist Lev Vygotsky [1896–1934] also argued for the developmental significance of symbolic play but from a social perspective. Vygotsky contended there is a zone of proximal development (ZPD), a level of ability the child has the potential to attain but cannot achieve without assistance ([1930–1935] 1978).

For Vygotsky, children's dramatic play provides indices of these zones of proximal development. For example, a child may be able pour tea from a toy teacup and cut slices from an imaginary cake before he or she is able to perform these actions with real china and real cutlery. Through dramatic play, the child conveys his or her readiness to learn new skills with the assistance of adults. While dramatic play may be a guide to a zone of proximal development for the adult, it certainly is not to the child. The child is playing for the sake of playing, not to give hints to the adult as to when and how the grown-up should intervene.

Although there has been a great deal of research on play since these theories were offered, we really have no new theories of play. However, we do know much more about the historical, social, and cultural variations of play.

© Jonathan A. Meyers

The Memory of Play

Frances Fowler recalls a memorable day from his childhood in the 1930s. After a long hard winter, a fantastic spring day arrived. Fowler and his brothers slipped away from their chores to fly kites. In the kitchen, his mother and sister became so entranced that they stopped their chores and went outside as well. His father and other farmers also put aside their work to watch the kites. Many neighbors came outdoors to join the fun. Fowler describes the scene this way:

There never was such a day for flying kites! God doesn't make two such days in a century. We played all our fresh line into the boys' kites and still they soared. We could hardly distinguish the tiny orange-colored specks. Now and then we slowly reeled one in, finally bringing it dipping and tugging to the earth, for the sheer joy of sending it up again. What a thrill to run with them, to the left and to the right, and see our poor earth-bound movements reflected minutes later in the majestic sky dance of the kites. We wrote wishes on slips of paper and slipped them over the string. Slowly, irresistibly they climbed until they reached the kites. Surely all those wishes would be granted.

We never knew where the hours went on that hilltop day. There were no hours, just a golden, breezy now. I think we were all a little beyond ourselves. Parents forgot their duty and their dignity; children forgot their combativeness and small spites. (Fowler 1949)

Although kites were not flown then for any other purpose than the sheer joy of flying them, they did have long-term meaning and value that could not have been predicted. During World War II, one of the boys who had flown the kites that day, according to Fowler, was in the service and returned home after more than a year as a prisoner of war. When asked about it, he said that when things got bad, he thought about the day the kites were flown. Similarly, a few years later, Fowler paid a sympathy call on a recently widowed woman who had been present on the day the kites were flown. When he offered his condolences, the woman smiled and said, "Henry had such fun that day. Do you remember the day we flew the kites?" (Fowler 1949).

Excerpt reprinted, by permission of the publisher, from F. Fowler, "The Day We Flew the Kites," *Reader's Digest*, August (1949). Originally published in *Parents Magazine*, May (1949). Used by permission.

Variations of play

Nicholas Orme describes play in medieval times (2001). During that period, play was looked upon as the defining characteristic of childhood and was regarded as primarily recreational and amusing. In a painting in 1559, the artist Breughel depicts more than two hundred children and adolescents playing with toys and taking part in games. For hundreds of years children's play—games, riddles, rhymes—was passed down by oral tradition from generation to generation (10 child generations to every three adult generations) (Opie & Opie 1959). This process continues today although to a much lesser extent.

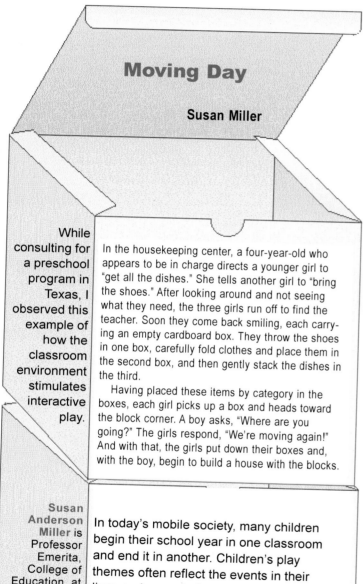

Moving Day

Susan Miller

While consulting for a preschool program in Texas, I observed this example of how the classroom environment stimulates interactive play.

In the housekeeping center, a four-year-old who appears to be in charge directs a younger girl to "get all the dishes." She tells another girl to "bring the shoes." After looking around and not seeing what they need, the three girls run off to find the teacher. Soon they come back smiling, each carrying an empty cardboard box. They throw the shoes in one box, carefully fold clothes and place them in the second box, and then gently stack the dishes in the third.

Having placed these items by category in the boxes, each girl picks up a box and heads toward the block corner. A boy asks, "Where are you going?" The girls respond, "We're moving again!" And with that, the girls put down their boxes and, with the boy, begin to build a house with the blocks.

Susan Anderson Miller is Professor Emerita, College of Education, at Kutztown University of Pennsylvania. She is also a consultant, columnist, and book author.

In today's mobile society, many children begin their school year in one classroom and end it in another. Children's play themes often reflect the events in their lives and are not always the neatly packaged themes, like the post office or pizza shop, that adults have planned for them. This scenario serves as an important reminder for educators to observe closely, listen carefully, and be available to provide materials and support to extend children's play in ways they find meaningful.

Play is a characteristic of children at all times and places. Nonetheless it varies with social class and culture. Sara Smilansky initiated a new line of play research studies with her finding that sociodramatic play was more common among children of advantage than it was among those with less advantage (1968). While some writers (Weinberger & Starkey 1994) contest this conclusion, they remain in the minority.

There are also cultural differences in play. One highly general finding is that the more complex the culture, the more complex the competitive games engaged in within that society (Sutton-Smith 1980). In addition, societies can be grouped according to collective versus competitive orientation. Again, more complex societies are more likely to be more competitive, and less complex societies, more collective (Sutton-Smith 1980).

At the early childhood level, however, there is likely much more similarity in children's play than difference across both culture and social class. This is true because young children are less socialized and more apt to create their own play than to adopt socially transmitted play activities. For the young, and to a degree all ages, play has personal meaning and value not dealt with in traditional theory and research.

Meaning and value of true play

With all these adult explanations and research findings regarding children's play, the point I am trying to make is that they are just that—adult explanations and descriptions. Adults look at children's play as, in one way or another, facilitating healthy development. Yet it is important to separate the functions and values adults attribute to children's play from the meaning and value that play has for the child. Brian Sutton-Smith devoted a long, productive career to the study of play and makes this point well:

> The definitions of play given by child players themselves generally center on having fun, being outdoors, being with friends, choosing freely, not working, pretending, enacting fantasy, drama, and playing games. There is little or no emphasis on the kind of growth that adults have in mind with their progress rhetoric. (Sutton-Smith 1997, 49)

I am not saying that play has no long-term developmental meaning or value. Instead, I maintain that play has a personal, experiential value of equal, if not greater, importance. A timeless article in *Reader's Digest*, "The Day We Flew the Kites," captures this value (see "The Memory of Play," p. 39).

On a wondrous day of kite flying, the people who participated did so for the sheer fun of it, not because it would benefit them at some future time. But they remembered the occasion, which demonstrates the well-known fact that we remember best those events

Where Are They Going?

Bonnie Kittredge

In mid-December I visited a Head Start program in a tiny Yupik Eskimo village on the west coast of Alaska. Everyone except me spoke Yupik, so I had to rely on visual clues as I watched the children absorbed in play.

The dramatic play area was set up like an office, with a nonfunctioning computer and keyboard. Three children wearing hard hats were sitting in chairs, one directly behind the other. The first of the three faced the computer screen and was making all kinds of hand motions. They sat in a row for perhaps 20 minutes.

When another child walked down the row of three, speaking with each one and pretending to write on an invisible notepad, I realized what I was observing. This child was a flight attendant taking drink orders. The first in the row was the pilot, the computer the cockpit. The other two children were passengers sitting quietly en route to somewhere. I chose not to interrupt the play to ask where they were going, so I was left to surmise—perhaps a trip to a basketball game in a neighboring village or to the doctor in Bethel, regional hub for the Kuskokwim Delta, about an hour's flight from this village.

The children of this village know lots more about small planes in which the pilots and their instruments are visible—as well as four-wheelers and snow machines—than they do about the kinds of transportation urban dwellers think of as common.

Courtesy Chefornak Head Start Program

Bonnie Kittredge, MS, is an early childhood consultant in Anchorage, Alaska, and a member of the staff development network at Teaching Strategies, Inc., in Washington, D.C.

---

that are connected with powerful emotions. Few will forget the time and place they first heard about the horror of 9/11. Fortunately, we also remember occasions, often associated with free play, of extreme happiness. When we are under stress or duress, recollections of happy moments provide comfort.

Keeping play memorable

As teachers of young children, we need to resist the pressures to transform play into work—into academic instruction. We encourage true play by making certain that we offer materials that leave room for the imagination—blocks, paints, paper to be cut and pasted—and that children have sufficient time to innovate with these materials. When we read to young children, we can ask them to make up their own stories or to give a different ending to the story they are hearing.

Giving children examples of how to use materials in innovative ways and then letting them experiment is important. Most of all we need to adopt a playful attitude that will encourage our children to do the same.

Given the times in which we live, we should afford children every opportunity to store as many happy recollections as they can. If we encourage and facilitate children's true play, we bequeath them an important and priceless gift, an *album of joyous memories.* Years from now these memories are what our young charges —grown up—will remember us by, and thank us for.

References

Brill, A.A., ed. 1938. *The basic writings of Sigmund Freud.* New York: Modern Library.

Fowler, F. 1949. The day we flew the kites. *Reader's Digest,* August.

Groos, K. 1898. *The play of animals.* New York: D. Appleton.

Groos, K. 1901. *The play of man.* New York: D. Appleton.

Montessori, M. [1912] 1964. *The Montessori method.* New York: Schocken.

Opie, I., & P. Opie. 1959. *The lore and language of school children.* New York: Oxford University Press.

Orme, N. 2001. *Medieval children.* New Haven: Yale University Press.

Piaget, J. 1951. *Play, dreams, and imitation in childhood.* Translated by F.M. Hodgson. Melbourne, Australia: Heinemann.

Smilansky, S. 1968. *The effects of socio-dramatic play on disadvantaged preschool children.* New York: Wiley.

Spencer, H. [1896] 1955. *Principles of psychology.* New York: D. Appleton.

Sutton-Smith, B. 1980. Children's play: Some sources of play theorizing. In *Children's play,* ed. K.H. Rubin. San Francisco: Jossey-Bass.

Sutton-Smith, B. 1997. *The ambiguity of play.* Cambridge, MA: Harvard University Press.

Vygotsky, L.S. [1930–1935] 1978. *Mind in society: The development of higher psychological processes.* Cambridge, MA: Harvard University Press.

Weinberger, L.A., & P. Starkey. 1994. Pretend play by African American children in Head Start. *Early Childhood Research Quarterly* 9: 327–43.

Janet K. Sawyers and Cosby S. Rogers

Helping Babies Play

Birth to 4 months

In these early months, babies explore their new world with their eyes. Things you can do to help this exploration are

- Provide bright, moving objects for babies to practice looking at. Mobiles should be interesting from the baby's view. Provide consistency by leaving the objects in their place so the baby begins to recognize familiar objects in the crib at home as well as in out-of-home care settings.

- Move objects close to and away from babies. Also, move your face close to and away from them. This will make a different visual impact than things that stay still. It helps babies judge the relationship between objects and between themselves and objects.

- Hold babies up to your shoulder and move them around to provide a better view.

- Show the baby in a mirror how beautiful and wonderful he is.

- Playfully engage the baby in repetitions of looking, smiling, talking, and laughing. The adult usually starts the game by smiling and talking to gain baby's attention. Experienced caregivers and mothers find that tongue clicking, head shaking, moving quickly toward baby and then stopping, and repeating certain sounds are entertaining to babies. Perform in a clownlike fashion and stop to wait for baby to do her part—laughing, smiling, or moving her arms and legs in excitement. Repeat the clown show several times, each time stopping for baby to have a turn. The show stops when baby starts to look away or shows other signs of fatigue, overstimulation, or lack of interest.

Babies explore sound and motion too. Some suggestions for increasing these explorations are

- Talk to babies in a playful way. Smile and repeat soft sounds—again, again. Stop between sounds and watch for them to smile or move in response to your voice. If you get a playful response, repeat the show.

- Sing to the baby. Make up songs just for this baby. Dance with the baby nestled on your shoulder.

- Play with the baby's hands and feet, gently patting and rubbing, saying silly, soft sounds to match. "Pedal" the baby's legs for a bike ride, describing where you're going.

Four to 8 months

In this stage, infants can use not only eyes and ears but hands and mouth to explore objects. Some ideas for this age group's play are

- Keep toy safety a primary concern. Provide objects that can be held by small hands but that are not small enough to fit entirely in the mouth. Toys must be washable and made of tough, durable materials. There must be no sharp edges or points that can injure and no small parts that can come off—small wheels or buttons, for example.

- Toys that move or make a sound in response to the baby's actions are best. Look for toys that pop up, turn, honk, rattle, or play music when the baby pushes, punches, hits, or pokes at them.

- Minimize interruptions to protect babies' exploration of new objects. Watch but don't interrupt when babies are busy exploring. Also prevent other children (especially older ones) from interrupting play. Having duplicates of several toys will help prevent would-be "snatchers" from robbing the explorer.

Babies are also becoming more social and enjoy your efforts to entertain them by

- playing "This Little Piggy Went to Market" with their toes and

- singing special songs while changing diapers and clothes or cutting nails.

Eight to 12 months

Babies now are fully active in exploring their world. Almost all babies crawl or creep; many walk around the room holding on, some are independently walking. Babies now combine objects and practice dropping, throwing, and squeezing. Some suggestions for fostering their play are

© Subjects & Predicates

• Provide objects to put in containers and dump out. Some good containers are plastic bowls, plastic storage boxes, baskets, and shoe boxes. Make sure that items to put in the containers are small enough for small hands but not small enough to fit entirely in the mouth. Good things to put in are small blocks, yarn balls, plastic lids, and rings from stack-a-ring toys.

• Hide objects for baby to find. Hide objects under covers. At first, leave part of the toy visible or cover with a see-through material (thin scarf, plastic lid, cheese cloth). Hide the baby under a cover—look and look until baby pops out, while asking, "Where's the baby? Where's Lucy?"

• Help babies practice sounds by repeating their sounds back—for example, *dada, oh oh,* and by the end of the first year, words like *kitty, baby,* and *doll.* Don't limit speech to imitating babies, but extend and expand their words into sentences.

• Read to the baby.

• Provide toys that challenge the infant's skills. Children this age practice pulling, pushing, poking, punching.

• Be sure toys are in working order. Toys that don't work are just no fun. They can be very frustrating.

• Introduce toys with more than one part. Infants this age especially like things that fit inside something else.

• Stretch baby's arms above her head, asking, "How big is baby? SOOOO big!" After a while, baby will hold her arms up alone to respond to your question.

• Play Pat-a-Cake, Peek-a-Boo, and Copycat with the baby.

• Children in this age group enjoy the sensory feeling of moving through space—riding piggyback, swinging in child-seat swings, riding in wagons, and dancing in an adult's arms. They and older babies also enjoy bouncing on an adult's knee to the accompaniment of a song or verse such as "This Is the Way the Lady Rides."

Twelve to 18 months

Infants in this age group are great experimenters, trying out all their skills this way and that just to see what will happen. The first pretend play occurs in this group when infants begin to act "as if" doing daily activities. They pretend to sleep, eat, or bathe. They then apply these acts to others and later copy others' behaviors as their own. Some suggestions for supporting play for these babies are

• Provide simple pictures of familiar items (laminated, covered with clear plastic, or put into zip-type plastic bags) for baby to practice naming.

• Read to the baby, talking about the book as you go.

• Provide safe places (indoors and outdoors) for moving—walking and climbing. Due to the likelihood of many falls, climbing steps should be plastic or covered with carpet. Tunnels and cabinets provide opportunities for going in, out, through, and under.

• Be the receiver of the child's pretend actions. Take a drink from the empty cup, smack your lips, and say, "Ummmm, good." Let the child comb your hair or pretend to wash your face. Then extend the pretense

© Marilyn Nolt

to another recipient such as a doll. Support the child's language development by narrating the drama as it progresses: "Jimmy is asleep," or "Oh, I'm going to be clean. I'm getting a bath."

• Provide real-looking toys for daily activities such as eating, bathing, riding, and cleaning. Important toys for pretense at this age are

Dolls (realistic, representative of a variety of racial/ethnic groups): daddy, mommy, brother, sister, baby.

Transportation vehicles: boats, planes, cars, trains.

Excerpted from Janet K. Sawyers and Cosby S. Rogers, *Helping Young Children Develop Through Play: A Practical Guide for Parents, Caregivers, and Teachers* (Washington, DC: NAEYC, 1988), 13–21.

Play Modifications for Children with Disabilities

© Ellen B. Senisi

Susan R. Sandall

Children with disabilities and other special needs may have difficulty participating in play activities. Teachers can use a variety of modifications and adaptations to help the child take part in and learn from play. These modifications and adaptations will be most useful when the teacher observes that the child is interested in the ongoing activities but is unable to fully participate.

The chart below identifies eight categories of curriculum modifications that teachers can use in their classrooms. Creative teachers will think of many other modifications. The critical steps are to observe the child's play and match the level of support to the child's need.

Susan R. Sandall, PhD, is an assistant professor at the University of Washington in Seattle. She is faculty advisor for the infant/toddler program and evaluation coordinator for the DATA (Developmentally Appropriate Treatment for Autism) project, both located in UW's Experimental Education Unit, an inclusive early childhood program.

Type of modification	Description	Examples
Environmental support	The teacher alters the physical, social, and/or temporal environment.	For a child who may wander from center to center, make a photo display of the centers so the child can select from the photos to make an individual schedule of what she plans to do.
Materials adaptation	The teacher modifies the play materials so that the child can manipulate them.	For a child who does not have the strength to stand for long periods of time, make a simple tabletop easel to let the child sit in a chair while painting.
Simplifying the activity	The teacher simplifies a complicated activity by breaking it into smaller parts or reducing the number of steps.	For the child who is interested in table games but overwhelmed by the parts and pieces, describe the steps in clear, simple terms and draw pictures for the child so she can follow the steps.
Using child preferences	The teacher uses the child's preferred material, activity, or person to encourage the child to play.	For the child who loves trains and has not yet explored the dramatic play area, develop a train station theme for the area or train-motif placemats in the housekeeping area.

Tea and Ironing in the Afternoon

Sabrina A. Brinson

One of my favorite play episodes happened when I was a preschool teacher at a program for children with special needs in Florida.

One afternoon the housekeeping center is buzzing with activity. ShaVonne, Kandi, and Andrette are seated at a round table chatting away. Suddenly they sit up and adjust their church hats. Bonnie teeters over to them in pink high heels carrying a teapot. She holds her pearls back as she leans forward to fill each of their cups, among nods and thank-yous. The church ladies' conversation continues, and Bonnie hurries back, balancing an imaginary tray of cookies—thin mints and lemon squares, from the looks of it.

Meanwhile, Jeremy's flowered hat slides down as he briskly irons clothes. Jeremy doesn't tend to talk a lot during activities because of a speech problem. He blows his bangs out of his face and hands a shirt to Reginald, who folds it and plops it on top of the pile. For the rest of the play period, they talk nonstop about their work.

Ding! The bell rings for cleanup. Crystal looks in the mirror and pats her red pillbox hat. Still smiling, she unclips the green plastic earrings that dangle to her shoulders and puts them away. Irene signals to Lucy, who is deaf, and they quickly put away the broom and mop. Eric takes his thumb out of his mouth to stack dishes, and Freddie plows over the area rug with the vacuum cleaner one last time. "Vacuum cleaner, vacuum cleaner, vacuum cleaner . . ." He repeats the words over and over while rolling it into the closet.

Sabrina A. Brinson, PhD, is an assistant professor of early childhood education at the University of Memphis in Tennessee. She has also been a preschool teacher and coordinator of an inclusive model preschool program.

Type of modification	Description	Examples
Special equipment	The teacher uses special or adaptive devices to allow the child's access to and participation in the activity.	For the child who uses a wheelchair, which places him at a different height than the other children, ask the therapist about using a beanbag chair for floor-time activities.
Adult support	The teacher or another adult in the classroom joins the child's play and encourages involvement through modeling and commenting.	For the enthusiastic child who is often on the verge of losing control, go to the play area and join the child's play to slow down the pace and talk about the children's play.
Peer support	The teacher uses peers and helps them join a child's play to give encouragement through modeling and commenting.	For the child who has difficulty with activities that require several steps (such as making a collage or building a castle), pair the child with a buddy. The two can then take turns participating in the activity.
Invisible support	The teacher arranges naturally occurring events within an activity to increase the probability of the child's success.	For the child who is not yet speaking or has difficulty making others understand, place photos or picture symbols in the play area so that the child can use them to increase peers' understanding.

Adapted, by permission of the publisher, from S.R. Sandall, I.S. Schwartz, G.E. Joseph, H.Y. Chou, E.M. Horn, J. Lieber, S.L. Odom, & R. Wolery, *Building Blocks for Teaching Preschoolers with Special Needs* (Baltimore: Paul H. Brookes 2002), 46.

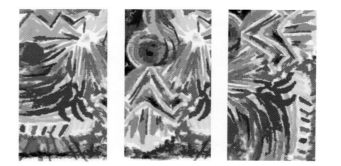

Beyond Banning War and Superhero Play
Meeting Children's Needs in Violent Times

Diane E. Levin

Four-year-old Jules is particularly obsessed. Telling him no guns or pretend fighting just doesn't work. When he's a good guy, like a Power Ranger, he thinks it's okay to use whatever force is needed to suppress the bad guy, "because that's what a superhero does!" And then someone ends up getting hurt. When we try to enforce a ban, the children say it's not superhero play, it's some other kind of play. Many children don't seem to know more positive ways to play, or they play the same thing over and over without having any ideas of their own. I need some new ideas.

This experienced teacher's account captures the kinds of concerns I often hear from teachers worried about how to respond to war play in their classrooms (Levin 2003). These expressions of concern about play with violence tend to increase when violent world events, like 9/11 and the war against Iraq, dominate the news.

Play, viewed for decades as an essential part of the early childhood years, has become a problem in many classrooms, even something to avoid. Teachers ask why play is deemed so important to children's development when it is so focused on fighting. Some are led to plan other activities that are easier to manage and appear at first glance to be more productive. Reducing playtime may seem to reduce problems in the short term, but this approach does not address the wide-ranging needs children address through play.

Diane E. Levin, PhD, is a professor of education at Wheelock College in Boston. For many years her work has focused on how to promote children's healthy development, learning, and behavior in violent times.

Children's art reproduced from *Helping Young Children Understand Peace, War, and the Nuclear Threat* © 1985 by Nancy Carlsson-Paige and Diane E. Levin, published by NAEYC. Illustrations above by Sandi Collins.

Why are children fascinated with war play?

There are many reasons why children bring violent content and themes into their play. They are related to the role of play in development and learning as well as to the nature of the society in which war play occurs (Carlsson-Paige & Levin 1987, 1990; Cantor 1998; Levin 1998a, 1998b, 2003; Katch 2001).

Exposure to violence. From both therapeutic and cognitive perspectives, children use play to work out an understanding of experience, including the violence to which they are exposed. Young children may see violence in their homes and communities as well as in entertainment and news on the screen. We should not be surprised when children are intent on bringing it to their play. Children's play often focuses on the most salient and graphic, confusing or scary, and aggressive aspects of violence. It is this content they struggle to work out and understand. Typically, the children who seem most obsessed with war play have been exposed to the most violence and have the greatest need to work it out.

Need to feel powerful. Most young children look for ways to feel powerful and strong. Play can be a safe way to achieve a sense of power. From a child's point of view, play with violence is very seductive, especially when connected to the power and invincibility portrayed in entertainment. The children who use war play to help them feel powerful and safe are the children who feel the most powerless and vulnerable.

Influence of toys linked to violent media.

Children's toys give powerful messages about the content and direction of play. Open-ended toys, like blocks, stuffed animals, and generic dinosaurs, can be used in many ways that the child controls. Highly structured toys, such as action figures that talk and playdough kits with molds to make movie characters, tend to have built-in features that show children how and what to play. Many of today's best-selling toys are of the highly structured variety and are linked to violent media. Such toys are appealing because they promise dramatic power and excitement. These toys channel children into replicating the violent stories they see on screen. Some children, like Jules, get "stuck" imitating media-linked violence instead of developing creative, imaginative, and beneficial play.

> **O**pen-ended toys, like blocks, stuffed animals, and generic dinosaurs, can be used in many ways that the child controls.

Teachers' concerns about war play

There are many reasons why teachers are concerned about war play and why they seek help figuring out how to deal with it.

Lack of safety in the classroom.
Play with violence tends to end up with children out of control, scared, and hurt. Managing aggressive play and keeping everyone safe can feel like a never-ending struggle and a major diversion from the positive lessons we want children to learn.

Old approaches not working.
Many veteran teachers say that the bans they used to impose on war play no longer work. Children have a hard time accepting limits or controlling their intense desire or need to engage in the play. And children find ways to circumvent the ban—they deny that play is really war play (that is, they learn to lie) or sneak around conducting guerilla wars the teacher does not detect (they learn to deceive).

Worries about the limited nature of the play.
Like Jules, some children engage in the same play with violence day after day and bring in few new or creative ideas of their own. Piaget called this kind of behavior imitation, not play (Carlsson-Paige & Levin 1987). These children are less likely to work out their needs regarding the violence they bring to their play or benefit from more sustained and elaborated play.

Concerns about lessons learned from the play.
When children pretend to hurt others, it is the opposite of what we hope they will learn about how to treat each other and solve problems. Children *learn* as they play—and what they play affects what they learn. When children are exposed to large amounts of violence, they learn harmful lessons about violence, whether they are allowed to play it in the classroom or not.

At the same time, children do not think about the violence they bring into their play in the same way adults do. Jules focuses on one thing at a time; he sees the bad guy as one dimensional without thinking about what makes him bad. He thinks good guys can do whatever hurtful things they want because they are good. Except when he gets carried away and hurts another child, Jules probably does know that at some level his play is different from the real violence he is imitating.

> **W**hen children are exposed to large amounts of violence, they **learn harmful lessons about violence,** whether they are allowed to play it in the classroom or not.

Reconciling children's needs and adults' concerns

In our society children are exposed to huge amounts of pretend and real violence. There are no simple or perfect solutions that simultaneously address children's needs and adults' concerns (Carlsson-Paige & Levin 1987). However, there is much teachers can do working with and outside of the play to make it better for everyone (see "Approaches to Working with Violent Play" and "Approaches to Working Outside Violent Play").

More important now than ever

There is no perfect approach for dealing with children's play with violence in these times. The best strategy is to vastly reduce the amount of violence children see. This would require adults to create a more peaceful world and limit children's exposure to media violence and toys marketed with media violence.

Given the state of the world, including the war against Iraq, children now more than ever need to find ways to work out the violence they see. For many, play helps them do so. We have a vital role in helping meet their needs through play. We must create an approach that addresses the unique needs of children growing up in the midst of violence as well as concerns of adults about how play with violence contributes to the harmful lessons children learn.

References

Cantor, J. 1998. *"Mommy, I'm scared!" How TV and movies frighten children and what we can do to protect them.* New York: Harcourt Brace.

Carlsson-Paige, N., & D.E. Levin. 1987. *The war play dilemma: Balancing needs and values in the early childhood classroom.* New York: Teachers College Press.

Carlsson-Paige, N., & D.E. Levin. 1990. *Who's calling the shots? How to respond effectively to children's fascination with war play and war toys.* Gabriola Island, BC, CAN: New Society.

Katch, J. 2001. *Under dead man's skin: Discovering the meaning of children's violent play.* Boston: Beacon.

Levin, D.E. 1998a. *Remote control childhood? Combating the hazards of media culture.* Washington, DC: NAEYC.

Levin, D.E. 1998b. Play with violence. In *Play from birth to twelve: Contexts, perspectives, and meanings,* eds. D. Fromberg & D. Bergin. New York: Garland.

Levin, D.E. 2003. *Teaching young children in violent times: Building a peaceable classroom.* 2nd ed. Cambridge, MA: Educators for Social Responsibility; Washington, DC: NAEYC.

Levin, D.E., & S. Linn. 2003. The commercialization of childhood. In *Psychology and consumer culture: The struggle for a good life in a materialistic world,* eds. T. Kasser & A.D. Kanner. Washington, DC: American Psychological Association.

Approaches to Working with Children's Violent Play

Address children's needs while trying to reduce play with violence. Banning play rarely works, and it denies children the opportunity to work out violence issues through play or to feel that their

interests and concerns are important. Trying to ban media-controlled imitative play, or even just contain it, can be an appropriate stopgap measure when problems become overwhelming. However, a total ban on this kind of play may leave children to work things out on their own without the guidance of adults.

Ensure the safety of all children. Involve children in developing rules for indoor and outdoor play that ensure safety. Help children understand the safety issues and what they can do to prevent injuries (physical and psychological) to themselves and others. Encourage children to paint, tell stories, and write (as they get older) to deal with issues of violence in ways that are safe and easier to control than play.

Promote development of imaginative and creative play (rather than imitative play). To work through deep issues and needs in a meaningful way, most children require direct help from adults. How you help depends on the nature of children's play (Levin 1998b). Take time to observe the play and learn what children are working on and how. Use this information to help children move beyond narrowly scripted play that focuses on violent actions. Help children gain skills to work out the violent content they bring to their play, learn the lessons you aim to teach, and move on to new issues.

Encourage children to talk with adults about media violence. As children struggle to feel safe and make sense of violence—regardless of the source—they need to know that we are there to help them with this process (Levin 2003). Start by trying to learn what they know, the unique meanings they have made, and what confuses and scares them.

When a child raises an issue, it is helpful to start by using an open-ended question like "What have you heard about that?" Respond based on what you learn about their ideas, questions, and needs. Keep in mind that children do not understand violence in or out of play as adults do. Try to correct misconceptions ("The planes that go over our school do not carry bombs"), help sort out fantasy and reality ("In real life people can't change back and forth like the Power Rangers do"), and provide reassurance about safety ("I can't let you play like that because it's my job to make sure everyone is safe").

• Try to reduce the impact of antisocial lessons that children learn both in and out of play. It can be helpful to encourage children to move from imitative to creative play so they can transform violence into positive behavior. Then talk with them about what has happened in their play ("I see Spiderman did a lot of fighting today. What was the problem?"). Help children to connect their own

firsthand positive experiences about how people treat each other to the violence they have seen ("I'm glad that in real life you could solve your problem with Mary by . . ."). These connections can help defuse some of the harmful lessons children learn about violence.

Talking with children about violence is rarely easy, but it is one of our most powerful tools. It is hard to predict the directions in which children might take the conversations, and teachers often find it challenging to show respect for the differing ways families try to deal with these issues.

Work closely with families. Reducing children's exposure to violence is one essential way to reduce their need to bring violence into their play. Most of young children's exposure to violence occurs in the home, so family involvement is vital. Through parent workshops and family newsletters that include resource materials such as those listed here, teachers can help families learn more about

how to protect children from violence, help children deal with the violence that still gets in, and promote play with open-ended toys and nonviolent play themes (Levin 1998a, 2003). In addition, families can learn about how to resist the advertising for toys linked to violence in ways that keep the peace in the family (Levin 1998a; Levin & Linn 2003).

Learning to Play Again

A Constructivist Workshop for Adults

Ingrid Chalufour, Walter F. Drew, and Sandra Waite-Stupiansky

I remember now how children love to play. I look around and see math and science things disguised as wire, wood and foam, bamboo, colored plastic rings, cardboard tubes, fabric, yarn, and many other things. Let me get my hands on them so I can play and learn and remember the child inside of me.

— W.F. Drew

Ingrid Chalufour is a project director at Education Development Center in Newton, Massachusetts. She has developed early childhood science materials (*Discovering Nature with Young Children,* with Karen Worth, from Redleaf Press). She has designed many professional development programs and courses focused on providing the experiences and support teachers and managers need to implement new learning in their classrooms and programs.

Walter F. Drew, EdD, early childhood consultant and trainer, founded the Institute for Self Active Education and the Reusable Resource Association, developing reusable resource/recycle centers to provide creative early childhood materials. Parents Choice Foundation named Dr. Drew's Discovery Blocks Best Toy in 1982. He is an adjunct faculty member at Brevard Community College in Melbourne, Florida.

Sandra Waite-Stupiansky, PhD, is professor of elementary education at Edinboro University of Pennsylvania, where she teaches early childhood undergraduate and graduate courses. She has been managing editor of the NAEYC Play, Policy, and Practice Interest Forum's newsletter, since 1995.

Photos courtesy of the authors.

Constructive, exploratory, and dramatic play are at the heart of early childhood education. Play experiences are key to children forming early understandings about the natural world, mathematical and early literacy ideas, and social competence. Yet in many early care and education programs and throughout our society, play is overlooked and undervalued.

When replicated for adults, hands-on play and reflection experiences lead to insights into children's learning and the teaching process. In the same way that children engage in the reverie of play, adults can rediscover the joy and importance of their own play and creativity.

This how-to article is a practical guide for conducting a dynamic, hands-on, adult play workshop. When provided with a carefully structured setting, open-ended materials, and a sensitive play coach, teachers—and parents—can refocus and rethink the role of play. The process often alters insights and changes approaches to the education of young children. The workshops apply constructivist principles to create a learning community in which adults build their own knowledge through hands-on play, reflection on their play experiences, and collaboration with peers.

This approach to teaching and learning is built on several guiding assumptions:

• Every child and adult has a developmental need to experience creativity and self-expression. Play with concrete, open-ended materials offers a powerful medium.

• Children and adults who are skilled at play with both things and ideas have more power, influence, and capacity to create meaningful lives. Play can build capacities like problem solving, persistence, and collaboration, which we draw on throughout our lives.

• Play is a powerful mode of response to new experiences in which the content and meaning are ambiguous and the outcome uncertain. A playful attitude enables the mind to remain open to explore and

Sample Outline for a Six-Hour Play Workshop

8:30 a.m.   **Refreshments**

9:00 a.m.   **Welcome**

9:30 a.m.   **Introduction.** The coach offers a few thoughts about play, the improvement of teaching and learning, the construction of knowledge, and creative expression. She or he introduces the first play activity.

9:45 a.m.   **Solitary Play, Sharing in Pairs, and Walk-About, Talk-About.** Participants engage in solo play, reflect on their play, and describe in some detail what they did. They look for connections between the construction of the outer pattern or design and inner knowledge and the curriculum.

Short Break

10:45 a.m.   **Large Group.** Participants and the coach discuss what happened. What is the value of this experience for the player? What are the implications for our work with children? What is the potential value for teachers and parents? For administrators? Does the play offer evidence of mathematical thinking, language development, or science concepts?

Drawing or Journal Entry

12:00 p.m.   **Lunch**

12:45 p.m.   **Cooperative Play and Follow-Up.** Small groups work with chosen materials and then discuss their creations. What value is this collaborative process in terms of moral development? What behaviors detract from the collaborative process? Can you identify any behaviors on your own part that you observed? Can you imagine a different way of collaborating? What implications do you see for the classroom?

1:45 p.m.   **Large Group Processing.** Participants discuss what they have learned about individual play and collaboration and compare experiences as individual players and as cocreators. Can you distinguish differences in how you operate and function? How can collaborative play be useful in your program? What have you observed about the value of open-ended materials?

2:15 p.m.   **Discussion: The Learning Experience—Observing, Reflecting, and Documenting.** What are the essential elements of the play experience? What is the role of the teacher in the process of reflecting and documenting?

2:45 p.m.   **Meditation Walk and/or Journal Entry.** In what way does play contribute to building community? Reflect on the content of your play: What meaning does it have for you?

3:15 p.m.   **Closing Comments and Questions.** A look at some action steps we can take together.

imagine a wider range of possibilities when seeking answers to new experiences.

• Play can and should be taught to children, teachers, and parents alike through direct experience. Teaching play requires setting the stage for learning by creating a safe, accepting environment for hands-on activities, reflection, and dialogue—as well as for investigating theory and practice.

• Play is an integral part of the curriculum, opening the door to more engaging, hands-on problem solving and inspiring projects. It is a natural organizing framework for integrating academic learning experiences in mathematics, science, literacy, and social studies.

• As children and adults play and work together, we can discuss differences of opinion and seek civilized ways of settling them. As we share emotions and thoughts, we gain insight into perspectives other than our own and discover that we are not so different from peers. This process helps us learn how to become positive, contributing members of the community.

The player's perspective

Imagine you have signed up for a play workshop. Soft piano music plays in the background as you and other participants enter the room. There are no chairs or tables, but distinct sets of various materials are on the floor—skeins of yarn, one-inch cardboard squares, and heaps of blue rectangles, green circles, yellow cylinders of foam, and so on. No scissors, staplers, or glue are in sight.

"Find a set of materials that appeals to you and a comfortable place to play on the floor," says the play coach. "Go with the flow, placing, arranging, stacking. Let the kinesthetic interaction move your mind into a focused state of relaxation and creative contemplation. There is nothing in particular you need to do with the materials—there is no product or goal. For the next 20 minutes or so, just relax and explore. During this time,

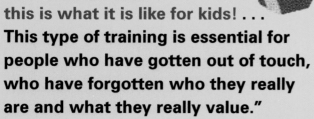

"**O**h, my goodness, this is what it is like for kids! . . . **This type of training is essential for people who have gotten out of touch, who have forgotten who they really are and what they really value.**"

please don't talk; just be with yourself. Also, instead of sharing, just use the materials you have chosen."

After your play experience, you and a colleague take turns describing your play. Then the facilitator asks if anyone wants to tell the whole group about the experience. People take turns describing their constructions. You walk around the room with the others, viewing what they have made. Each construction, like each play experience, is different.

One player admits, "Well, at first I was inhibited—it's like, I don't have any glue or scissors, so I can't do anything. But then I relaxed and got into just playing with the pieces."

With the excitement of a four-year-old, another says, "Hey! Look at me! I'm an architect! No, maybe an engineer—well, certainly a builder. I built a bridge across the pond, and now I can go fishing anytime I want. It was hard work constructing that bridge. I had to carefully measure, compare, sort, and then place materials alongside and on top of one another so my structure would be safe and strong."

A teacher who chose plastic caps as her medium says, "I experienced the same problem-solving skills that I've been teaching children for years. I was so aware of the sequencing, patterning, and problem solving that I was doing—it was like having a bell go off in my head. I knew I had to share this experience with other teachers."

"I see the need for play like this as part of the training process," says another player. "This fits the schema of what I want my staff to experience. I want them to create a personal vision for themselves based on direct experience."

Repeatedly you hear colleagues talk about focus, control, imagination, and self-expression through objects and open-ended materials. The construction of knowledge through direct experience, reflection, and social interaction takes on new meaning. Discussing your actions, thoughts, and feelings allows you to review the sensory experience, focusing first on the play materials and then gradually connecting with earlier life experiences or thoughts about the world. You make important connections between this experience and what you have read about constructivist learning.

Workshop events are a series of experiences that build on each other, each contributing to the growth of new understandings about teaching and learning. If we have convinced you that a play workshop is worth trying with a group of teachers or parents, you may want to use the following guidelines to prepare. The workshop can be a half day or a full day (see pp. 51 and 56 for sample outlines of each).

Role of the coach

The key to successful play experiences is the coach, who facilitates each player's process of connecting with imagination and self-expression. The coach trusts the players to make the most of their play experiences and to bring insight to their reflections.

The coach sets the stage by creating an environment in which people feel safe and accepted. The room should be wide open, empty, well lit, and preferably carpeted. Each person needs enough space to spread out and make expanding patterns or large structures without being crowded by neighbors. Soft background music enhances the mood (see suggestions on p. 55). Participants can relax and focus their attention easily and engage in conversation without fear of being evaluated and judged.

The coach selects a wide variety of open-ended manipulative resources that discourage competition and comparison. Recycled materials are perfect; businesses everywhere throw away potentially fabulous play materials. Clay, paint, blocks, and sand also can be used, as can nifty finds from thrift shops and yard sales. Each set of materials must be abundant, permitting

repetition and elaboration of physical patterns, the development of systems, and the continued flow of an idea or pattern over and over again. There should be more sets available than there are participants.

On the floor throughout the room, the coach arranges the materials in attractive sets, making them easy to distinguish, select, focus on, and use in creative constructive play. No telephones, loud noises, people talking, or other distractions that disturb play and contemplation are permitted.

During the workshop the coach maintains a balance between setting limits, observing, listening, and engaging in interactions that communicate acceptance and validate the participants' contributions. Rules such as no talking and no sharing of materials contribute to the feeling of safety needed by players to connect with their inner creativity. Sound, motion, judgment, criticism, and competition all have the power to counter the productive focus of play. The intent is to ensure a concrete, creative, and enjoyable experience and then to encourage reflection by inviting participants to talk about their experiences.

Some initial uncertainty, disorientation, and settling down can be expected. The coach knows that participants will settle in and become purposefully engaged. There is inevitably a moment in the play when things come together.

Through observation and reflection, a coach becomes sensitive to the style and pace of effective interactions—when to ask questions, which questions to ask, what action might best guide a player's progress, what comment or question might lead to new insight.

> *"I really feel that [the play workshop] has helped our teachers understand the children, the environment, and children's play. I can really see it when the teachers play with the children, when they talk to them, when they are setting up the environment, when they are figuring out what materials they want to bring to the classroom."*

Conducting the workshop

Like young children, the adults in a play workshop progress from solitary, parallel play to cooperative play. The coach facilitates this process in the following ways.

Solitary (solo) play

• Introduce the participants, then say a few words about the concept of play, review the workshop schedule, and introduce the first activity. Let players know there is no hidden agenda nor any expected outcome.

• Allow approximately 20 minutes for the solitary play experience. Ask participants to choose and play with one set of materials, to just fiddle and follow an inspiration or insight. Request that they not to talk.

• Give a five-minute warning so participants can finish what they are doing. If anyone wants to continue exploring beyond the allotted time, let him do so.

• Ask participants to find a buddy and take three to five minutes each to tell one another about their play experiences. One person should speak while the other listens. The speaker has maximum opportunity to express thoughts, feelings, and experiences—to think out loud—and relate the content of the play experience spontaneously.

• Ask participants to each create a journal, a visual or written representation of his work as a part of the reflection process. "Draw a picture of what you made. What did you see? What happened?" Players can draw one part of the pattern or the entire construction. The depiction can be reprensenational or abstract. Encourage players who choose to write about the experience to simply describe what they did. "Watch what happens as you think and review your play experiences."

• Invite willing participants to share their play experiences with the larger group, describing what they did and what happened to them. Ask them to note any rela-

tionships they see between the physical patterns they created and their personal style. For example, "I made a repeating pattern, each repeat in a different color. I'm a very organized person, and I don't like surprises"

• Encourage participants to become increasingly aware of the power of play and the diversity of human style and expression. Prompt comments by asking open-ended questions like "Is there anything you would like to share about your play experience?" Follow-up comments, "You balanced the blocks carefully" or "Could you tell me about your choice of colors?" can draw out more information.

• Lead participants in a Walk-About, Talk-About activity so they can see and discuss the various creations in the room.

• Lead a group discussion about the relationships between participants' play experiences and their work with children and other adults. To get started, ask questions such as

What have you learned from this experience?

What assumptions can we make about play?

What is the relationship between your play experience and children's development in the physical, emotional, cognitive, and social realms?

What are the implications of using this experience with children and other adults—parents, teachers?

What is the teacher's role in facilitating rich play experiences for children?

How might this experience influence play in your classroom?

Do you have thoughts on conducting the reflective process with children?

• Comment on players' references and inferences; invite them to discuss implications and consider strategies for improving and using the art of play.

Cooperative play

• Have participants form small groups, select a variety of materials, and work together to build a common structure.

• Allow time for reflecting within the small groups. Each member should have an opportunity to share thoughts and feelings, all of which are accepted as valid personal accounts.

• Lead the Walk-About, Talk-About, modeling how to be sensitive to each group member. Allow everyone to talk about the experience from his or her perspective—what each did, how it felt, what the participant learned, what insights or difficulties arose.

• Encourage sharing among the whole group so players can discuss what they learned. Pose questions about distinctions between parallel and cooperative play, the qualities of effective team behavior, diversity in the team process, and individual participation in teamwork/play. Note that insights gained through sharing and contrasting individual play and cooperative play experiences lead team members to work more effectively together.

• Summarize by helping players think about the relevance of the workshop to their work with children.

Classroom application

Coaches find that play workshops exert a profound effect on participants. Teachers often modify their classrooms after play experiences, looking for new materials and ways to display them. They develop new appreciation for open-ended materials and want to provide children with a greater quantity and variety. They scrounge through their closets for old stashes of stuff that becomes new play material. They scour school- and community-based recycling/reuse programs, thrift shops, and tag sales.

Beth, an early childhood special education teacher in Brevard County, Florida, was inspired after a play workshop. She relates, "I gathered a variety of materials from our local resource center—squishy foam, odd-shaped plastic pieces, flexible colored tubes, felt circles, metallic gaskets, and other discarded items donated by businesses. My goal was to inspire investigation, creative thinking, and the development of inventive language skills. . . . I simply said [to the children]: 'Here are some materials that I know you have never seen before. Play with them, move them around, and explore them and see what you discover!'"

Beth describes how she "observed and photographed the children and transcribed their comments as they worked in small groups investigating, comparing, and talking about the different attributes or properties of materials."

She found that the children worked together to create categories and systems for organizing and refining their higher-order thinking skills. For example, she says, "I placed long, colored shoelaces on the floor for them to use as 'sorting loops' to help them physically group the objects. It became a game and a way for me to informally assess their thinking and the language they constructed. After a while I asked, 'What have you discovered?'

"The children responded, 'These are different colors, but they both roll' and 'One of these is soft and one is hard, but they are both white.' I asked if they could show how the objects can be part of two sets by overlapping the sorting loops: 'Is there another way to group them?' The children discovered that some of the materials can be part of two or more sets. They had fun learning through play how to observe and compare, describe and classify.

"This hands-on, integrated approach to mathematics and science using concrete objects really helps children develop organizing and classification skills."

Suggested Music

Crystal Voices, *Sounds of Light*

Incantation, *Remembrance*

Keith Jarrett, *The Melody at Night, With You*

Michael Jones, *Magical Child, Piano Scapes,* and *Air Born*

Gary Lamb, *A Walk in the Garden, Angel, The Language of Love, Watching the Night Fall, Twelve Promises*

Various artists, *Celtic Twilight, Vol. 3: Lullabies*

Various artists, *Raga Taranga*

George Winston, *Autumn, Summer, Winter into Spring*

Connecting play to science, math, and literacy learning

The growing emphasis on standards and outcomes in early childhood education is pushing us to pay closer attention to academic subjects. What is appropriate for young children? How can content be taught in a manner that respects what we know about early development and the importance of play in the learning process?

The Education Development Center in Newton, Massachusetts, a project funded by the National Science Foundation, has been tackling this question on the science front for four years. The work, published by Redleaf Press and Heinemann (see Chalufour & Worth 2003 and Worth & Grollman 2003 on p.60), is built on the premise that development of reasoned theories for why and how things happen in the world is an important part of a quality early childhood education. The project's approach to science teaching begins with a rich set of experiences with materials and phenomena but also includes many varied opportunities for chil-dren's reflection on those experiences. Children are guided in drawing the data from their experiences and using the drawings as evidence as they form reasoned theories about how and why particular phenomena occur.

For example, we know that experiences with construction—with blocks and other manipulatives—provide an experiential base for children to build scientific understanding. But young children are capable of much more than experiencing the forces of gravity while building; they are also capable of forming theories about how and why their buildings are staying up or falling down. Why does foam work as a foundation on Juan's building but not on Janet's? What will happen if the green block is removed from George and Janelle's bridge? What is the best kind of material for a roof, and why?

As a Boston kindergarten teacher explains, "Sure, I asked, 'Tell me about your castle. Who lives there?' . . . but I never went further. Now I always ask, 'How come that is standing and this one keeps falling over?' or 'How come your structure fell down when you put that block on top? What do you think would happen if . . . ?' It's not like you need special materials; rather, it's a way

Sample Outline for a Half-Day Play Workshop

9:00 a.m. **Welcome and Brief Introduction**

9:30 a.m. **Silent Solo Play.** As participants play with one chosen material, the coach moves quietly about the room observing, careful not to disturb the play.

10:00 a.m. **Reflection.** Through writing and/or drawing, participants describe the material used, what they did with it, and what happened.

10:15 a.m. **Sharing One-on-One.** Players take turns sharing play experiences with a partner who listens carefully.

10:30 a.m. **Walk-About, Talk-About.** A brief, informal viewing of structures is followed by large-group debriefing. The coach responds to participants' comments and questions about their play.

11:00 a.m. **Cooperative Play.** The coach observes and facilitates play in small groups.

11:30 a.m. **Journal/Drawing Reflection.** Participants describe materials, what they did, and what happened.

11:45 a.m. **Large-Group Sharing.** Players and coach discuss what happened and what is needed to apply this practice in classrooms, staff development workshops, and family-education programs.

12:15 p.m. **Reflection and Journaling**

12:30 p.m. **Closing Comments**

of asking questions and observing kids and really furthering their thinking."

Math and literacy can be integrated into play experiences, especially in extended explorations and projects. Key to the inquiry process is recording data and using math processes regularly to describe and document observations like the measurement of buildings. Throughout, language plays an important role and has a powerful connection to conceptual learning.

Pat, an elementary teacher, participated in a play workshop. She then applied her new insights to the classroom curriculum. The children were interested in space exploration, so she gathered reusable resources (foam, wood, bottles, plastic bags, bamboo, cosmetic caps, cardboard) for the construction of a space station. In four groups of six children, science, mathematics, and literacy merged into sophisticated cognitive processes. Learning moved from cooperative three-dimensional construction to sharing and debriefing conversations and journaling and drawing.

Ryan's drawings and labels expressed his insight and excitement. "We had an energy transporter, space probe launcher, escape pod, training camps, intergalactic positioning system, information center, living quarters, space lab, landing platform, and power storage! It is meant to live in and study space."

Conclusion

The play workshop's format mirrors the way children learn about the world—that is, by constructing knowledge from experience. The physical models or structures are catalysts; they organize and focus the mind on elements that are concrete. Richness and clarity come from connecting creations with reflective dialogue.

Adult play workshops are invaluable professional development tools. They provide opportunities to

explore the role of the teacher in the learning process. Participants practice new ways of implementing a learner-centered approach to teaching and strategies for expanding on the interests and ideas that emerge from the constructive, exploratory, and dramatic play of children.

gain insight into the role reflection plays in children's learning. Participants engage in guided discussion, share their experiences with colleagues, and relate them to the teaching and learning process. As they step back and examine the process, they gain a deeper understanding of the role these processes can play in children's development and learning.

develop a reflective teaching practice. Coaching and questioning stimulate reflective thinking and deepen analytical skills, preparing teachers for using this kind of reflection as a consistent part of their assessment and planning process.

construct, implement, and evaluate new approaches to teaching. Participants play and work together in collaborative teams, developing new collegial relationships, powerful new teaching strategies, and insight into the role of documentation in assessment and planning.

Parent participants look on their children's play with new appreciation and re-evaluate their own roles in stimulating play in the home. They begin to question the amount of television viewing they allow and the kinds of toys they provide. One parent returned home from a workshop and cleaned out her children's closets, eliminating toys that did not encourage creative expression.

Print and Online Resources That Spotlight Young Children and Play

Compiled with the assistance of Alice S. Honig, Tammy Mann, and Susan Miller

Print resources

Althouse, R. 1994. *Investigating mathematics with young children.* New York: Teachers College Press.

Anderson, S.J. 2002. He's watching! The importance of the onlooker stage of play. *Young Children* 57 (6): 58.

Bergen, D., ed. 1987. *Play as a medium for learning and development: A handbook of theory and practice.* Portsmouth, NH: Heinemann.

Bergen, D.K. 2001. Pretend play and young children's development. ERIC Clearinghouse on Elementary and Early Childhood Education. ERIC Digests, EDO-PS-01-10. Online: www.ericeece.org/pubs/digests/2001/bergen01.html

Bergen, D., R. Reid, & L. Torelli. 2001. *Educating and caring for very young children: The infant/toddler curriculum.* New York: Teachers College Press.

Boyatzis, C.J. 1997. Of Power Rangers and V-chips. *Young Children* 52 (7): 74–79.

Bronson, M.B. 1995. *The right stuff for children birth to 8: Selecting play materials to support development.* Washington, DC: NAEYC.

Cain, B., & C. Bohrer. 1997. Battling Jurassic Park: From a fascination with violence toward constructive knowledge. *Young Children* 52 (7): 71–73.

Alice Sterling Honig, PhD, Professor Emerita of child development at Syracuse University, has annually conducted the week-long National Quality Workshop in June for nearly 30 years. A consultant for many child care programs, Dr. Honig is the author of more than a dozen books and nearly 400 articles and chapters.

Tammy Mann, PhD, currently serves as the director of the Early Head Start National Resource Center at Zero to Three, a national nonprofit organization that focuses on the importance of the first three years of life for later development.

Susan A. Miller, EdD, is Professor Emerita of early childhood education at Kutztown University of Pennsylvania. An international consultant and author, she is also a columnist for Scholastic.

Carter, M., & D. Curtis. 1995. *Training teachers: A harvest of theory and practice.* St. Paul, MN: Redleaf.

Chalufour, I., & K. Worth. 2003. *Discovering nature with young children.* St. Paul, MN: Redleaf. Available from NAEYC.

Chenfeld, M.B. 2002. *Creative experiences for young children.* 3rd ed. Portsmouth, NH: Heinemann.

Christie, J.F., ed. 1991. *Play and early literacy development.* Albany: State University of New York Press.

Christie, J., & F. Wardle. How much time is needed for play? *Young Children* 47 (3): 28–32.

Church, E.B. 1992. *Learning through play: Problem solving.* Learning through Play series [also available: *Science,* S.B. Kleinsinger; *Dramatic play,* eds. N. Hereford & J. Schall; *Blocks,* E.B. Church; *Art,* eds. N.J. Hereford & J. Schall; *Language,* S.A. Miller; *Math,* S. Waite-Stupiansky; *Music and Movement,* E.B. Church; *Sand, water, clay, and wood,* S.A. Miller]. New York: Scholastic Professional Books.

Cooper, J., & M. Dever. 2001. Sociodramatic play as a vehicle for curriculum integration in first grade. *Young Children* 56 (3): 58–63.

Council for Physical Education and Children. 2001. Recess in elementary schools. A position paper from the National Association for Sport and Physical Education. Online: www.aahperd.org/naspe/pdf_files/pos_papers/current_res.pdf.

DeBord, K., L.L. Hestenes, R.C. Moore, N. Cosco, & J.R. McGinnis. 2002. Paying attention to the outdoor environment is as important as preparing the indoor environment. *Young Children* 57 (3): 32–35.

Flynn, L.L., & J. Kieff. 2002. Including everyone in outdoor play. *Young Children* 57 (3): 20–27.

Ford, S. 1993. The facilitator's role in children's play. *Young Children* 48 (6): 66–69.

Forman, G., & D. Kuschner. 1983. *The child's construction of knowledge: Piaget for teaching children.* Washington, DC: NAEYC.

Fosnot, C.T. 1989. *Enquiring teachers, enquiring learners: A constructivist approach for teaching.* New York: Teachers College Press.

Froebel, F. [1826/1887] 2001. *The education of man.* Translated by W.N. Hailmann. Reprint, Grand Rapids, MI: Kindergarten Messenger.

Fromberg, D.P. 2001. *Play and meaning in early childhood education.* Boston: Allyn & Bacon.

Fromberg, D.P., & D. Bergen, eds. 1998. *Play from birth to twelve and beyond: Contexts, perspectives, and meanings.* New York: Garland.

Frost, J., S. Wortham, & S. Reifel. 2001. *Play and child development.* Upper Saddle River, NJ: Merrill/Prentice Hall.

Gardner, H. 1983. *Frames of mind: The theory of multiple intelligences.* New York: Basic.

Gowen, J. 1995. Research in Review. The early development of symbolic play. *Young Children* 50 (3): 75–84.

Greenberg, P. 1992. Creating creative play opportunities. *Young Children* 47 (5): 51.

Griffin, C., & B. Rinn. 1998. Enhancing outdoor play with an obstacle course. *Young Children* 53 (3): 18–23.

Hill, D.M. 1977. *Mud, sand, and water.* Washington, DC: NAEYC.

Hirsch, E.S., ed. 1996. *The block book.* 3rd ed. Washington, DC: NAEYC.

Honig, A.S. 1982. *Playtime learning games for young children.* Syracuse, NY: Syracuse University Press.

Honig, A.S. 1988. Research in Review. Humor development in children. *Young Children* 43 (4): 60–73.

Honig, A.S. 2001. Promoting creativity, giftedness, and talent in young children in preschool and school situations. In *Promoting creativity across the life span,* eds. M. Bloom & T.P. Gullotta. Washington, DC: Child Welfare League of America.

Howes, C., & S. Ritchie. 2002. *A matter of trust: Connecting teachers and learners in the early childhood classroom.* New York: Teachers College Press.

Hughes, F.P., J. Elicker, & L.C. Veen. 1995. A program of play for infants and their caregivers. *Young Children* 50 (2): 52–58.

Hughes, F. 2003. Sensitivity to the social and cultural contexts of the play of young children. In *Major trends and issues in early childhood education: Challenges, controversies, and insights,* 2nd ed., eds. J.P. Isenberg & M.R. Jalongo. New York: Teachers College Press.

Isenberg, J.P., & M.R. Jalongo. 2000. *Creative expression and play in early childhood.* 3rd ed. New York: Prentice Hall College Division.

Jensen, B.J., & J.A. Bullard. 2002. The mud center: Recapturing childhood. *Young Children* 57 (3): 16–19.

Jarrett, O.S. 2002. Recess in elementary school: What does the research say? ERIC Clearinghouse on Elementary and

Early Childhood Education. ERIC Digest, EDO-PS-02-5.

Johnson, J.E., J.F. Christie, & T.D. Yawkey. 1999. *Play and early childhood development.* 2nd ed. New York: Longman.

Jones, E., ed. 1993. *Growing teachers: Partnerships in staff development.* Washington, DC: NAEYC.

Jones, E., & G. Reynolds. 1990. *Master players.* New York: Teachers College Press.

Jones, E., & G. Reynolds. 1992. *The play's the thing: Teachers' roles in children's play.* New York: Teachers College Press.

Kalata, P. 1998. Parents! Let's play! *Young Children* 3 (5): 40–41.

Klemm, B. 1995. Viewpoint #1: Video-game violence. *Young Children* 50 (5): 53–55.

Klugman, E., & S. Smilansky, eds. 1990. *Children's play and learning: Perspectives and policy implications.* New York: Teachers College Press.

Lerner, C., with A. Dombro & K. Levine. 2000. *The magic of everyday moments: 0–4 months.* Booklet series [also available: *4–6 months; 6–9 months; 9–12 months; 12–15 months*]. Washington, DC: Zero to Three. Online: www.zerotothree.org/magic/main.html.

Lytle, D.E., ed. 2003. *Play and educational theory and practice.* Vol. 5 of *Play and culture studies.* Westport, CT: Greenwood.

McCracken, J.B. 1999. *Playgrounds: Safe and sound.* Brochure. Washington, DC: NAEYC.

McCracken, J.B. 2000. *Play is FUNdamental.* Brochure. Washington, DC: NAEYC. Available in Spanish.

McDermott, K. 1999. Helping primary school children work things out during recess. *Young Children* 54 (4): 82–84.

McGinnis, J.R. 2002. Enriching the outdoor environment. *Young Children* 57 (3): 28–31.

McNiff, S. 1998. *Trust the process: An artist's guide to letting go.* Boston: Shambhala.

NAEYC. 1990. NAEYC position statement on media violence in children's lives. *Young Children* 45 (5): 18–21. Online: www.naeyc.org/resources/position_statements/psmevi98.htm.

NAEYC. 1998. *Media violence and children: A guide for parents.* Brochure. Washington, DC: NAEYC.

NAEYC. 1999. *Toys: Tools for learning.* Brochure. Washington, DC: NAEYC. Available in Spanish.

National Association of Early Childhood Specialists in State Departments of Education. 2002. Recess and the importance of play: A position statement on young children and recess. Online: http://ericps.crc.uiuc.edu/naecs/position/recessplay.html.

NCTA (National Cable Television Association). 1996. The National Television Violence Study key findings and recommendations. *Young Children* 51 (3): 54–55.

Nourot, P.M., & J.L. Van Hoorn. 1991. Research in Review. Symbolic play in preschool and primary settings. *Young Children* 46 (6): 40–50.

Owocki, G. 2002. *Literacy through play.* Portsmouth, NH: Heinemann. Available from NAEYC.

Paley, V.G. 1992. *The boy who would be a helicopter: The uses of storytelling in the classroom.* Cambridge, MA: Harvard University Press.

Paley, V.G. 1991. *You can't say you can't play.* Cambridge, MA: Harvard University Press.

Pellegrini, A., & J. Perlmutter. 1988. Rough and tumble play on the elementary school playground. *Young Children* 43 (2): 14–17.

Reynolds, G., & E. Jones. 1997. *Master players: Learning from children at play.* New York: Teachers College Press.

Rivkin, M.S. 1995. *The great outdoors: Restoring children's right to play outside.* Washington, DC: NAEYC.

Rogers, C.S., & J.K. Sawyers. 1988. *Play in the lives of children.* Washington, DC: NAEYC.

Saracho, O.N., & B. Spodek, eds. 1998. *Multiple perspectives on play in early childhood education.* Albany: State University of New York Press.

Segal, M. 1998. *Your child at play—Birth to one year: Discovering the senses and learning about the world.* 2nd ed. Your Child at Play series [also available: *One to two years; Two to three years; Three to five years; Five to eight years*]. New York: New Market.

Sheridan, M.K., G.M. Foley, & S.H. Radlinski. 1995. *Using the supportive play model: Individualized intervention in early childhood practice.* New York: Teachers College Press.

Stephenson, A. 2002. What George taught me about toddlers and water. *Young Children* 57 (3): 10–15.

Stone, S.J. 1995. Wanted: Advocates for playing in the primary grades. *Young Children* 50 (6): 45–54.

Stupiansky, S.W. 1992. *Math: Learning through play.* New York: Scholastic.

Stone, S.J. 1995. Wanted: Advocates for playing in the primary grades. *Young Children* 50 (6): 45–54.

Sutton-Smith, B. 1980. *Play and learning.* New York: Wiley.

Szamreta, J.M. 2003. Peekaboo power: To ease separation and build secure relationships. *Young Children* 58 (1): 88–94.

Thompson, S., P. Knudson, & D. Wilson. 1997. Helping primary children with recess play: A social curriculum. *Young Children* 52 (6): 17–21.

Van Hoorn, J., P.M. Nourot, B. Scales, & K.R. Alward. 2003. *Play at the center of the curriculum.* 3rd ed. Upper Saddle River, NJ: Merrill/Prentice Hall.

Vygotsky, L.S. [1966] 1976. Play and its role in the mental development of the child. In *Soviet developmental psychology,* ed. M. Cole, 76–99. White Plains, NY: M.E. Sharpe.

Williamson, G.G., & M.E. Anzalone. 2001. *Sensory integration and self-regulation in infants and toddlers: Helping very young children interact with their environment.* Washington, DC: Zero to Three.

Worth, K., & S. Grollman. 2003. *Worms, shadows, and whirlpools: Science in the early childhood classroom.* Portsmouth, NH: Heinemann. Available from NAEYC.

Ziegler, E.F., D.G. Singer, & S.J. Bishop-Josef, eds. 2004. *Children's play: The roots of reading.* Washington, DC: Zero to Three. Available from NAEYC.

Online resources

American Academy of Pediatrics lists several good resources on selecting safe, appropriate toys; search for *toys.* **www.aap.org**

The Association for the Study of Play holds an annual conference and publishes the *Annual Volume of Play and Culture Studies.* **www.csuchico.edu/phed/tasp**

Consumer Product Safety Commission advises about toy selection and provides safety alerts about products on the market. Also in Spanish. **www.cpsc.gov**

International Association for the Child's Right to Play (IPA) offers its *Declaration of the Child's Right to Play* and publishes the quarterly newsletter *PlayRights.* **www.ncsu.edu/ipa/index.html**

The Lion and Lamb Project works to stop the marketing of violence to children through guides, training, and advocacy. **www.lionlamb.org**

National Lekotek Center makes play accessible to children with disabilities. Play and learning centers for children and families are located throughout the country. **www.lekotek.org**

Playing for Keeps promotes healthy, constructive, nonviolent play for all children. Board members come from the toy industry and early childhood education. **www.playingforkeeps.org**

Talking to Kids about War and Violence (PBS Parents Website) helps adults answer children's questions about violence and respond to their feelings of stress in age-appropriate ways. (Also in Spanish) **www.pbs.org/parents/issuesadvice/war/**

Teachers Resisting Unhealthy Children's Entertainment (TRUCE) prepares an annual *Toy Action Guide* and *Media Violence and Children Action Guide* for parents and teachers of young children. **www.truceteachers.org**

Zero to Three Web site provides tips on play; in Parenting A–Z, click on *P* and scroll down to Play. **www.zerotothree.org/ztt_parentAZ.html**

Reflecting, Discussing, Exploring

Questions and Follow-Up Activities

Marilou Hyson

The articles in *Spotlight on Young Children and Play* represent just a small sample of the many valuable resources for early childhood educators interested in children's play and its contributions to development and learning. For students in early childhood professional preparation programs, for early childhood teachers taking part in training and other forms of professional development, and for individuals seeking to broaden their understanding of this important topic, we hope these articles and the accompanying professional development resources (pp. 58–59) will open doors to further exploration of the power and potential of children's play.

To help you reflect on and apply insights from these articles, we have developed a series of questions and suggested follow-up activities. The series begins with an invitation to think about your own early experiences with play. Specific questions and suggested activities related to each article follow. Finally, we help you pull things together with general questions about curriculum, teaching practices, resources, and next steps.

Marilou Hyson, PhD, is NAEYC's associate executive director for professional development.

A. Recalling your own early experiences

1. What memories do you have of early experiences with play? What are your very first play memories? What did you play? With what did you play? With whom did you play?

2. Share your play memories with family, co-workers, or fellow students, including those of different generations and cultures. What similarities and differences do you find? How do these discussions help you better understand children's play?

B. Expanding on each article

"Chopsticks and Counting Chips: Do Play and Foundational Skills Need to Compete for the Teacher's Attention in an Early Childhood Classroom?"/*Elena Bodrova and Deborah J. Leong*

The authors, codevelopers of the Tools of the Mind curriculum and research project, point out that children's play helps children learn foundational skills that set the stage for later academic learning.

1. The school principal described at the beginning of this article thinks that children should play at home and come to school to learn. After reading the article, and drawing on your experience, how would you respond to the principal?

2. The authors' ideas about play have been highly influenced by the theories of Russian psychologist Lev Vygotsky. Think about Vygotsky's ideas about play's importance, then consider or discuss with others times when you have witnessed those benefits and what teachers were doing to scaffold children's play.

3. The authors focus on sociodramatic or pretend play. What are the reasons this kind of play is especially important for children's development of self-regulation and symbolic thought?

4. In your own teaching, try some of the play-scaffolding strategies described by the authors. If possible, discuss your successes and challenges with others.

"The Bugs Are Coming! Improvisation and Early Childhood Teaching"/*Carrie Lobman*

The author—who is also an improv comedian—asks early childhood educators to celebrate and build on the unexpected, wacky, playful moments that happen every day in our work with young children.

5. The article begins with a wonderful example of the unpredictable moments that occur in early childhood classrooms. From your experience as a teacher, student, or parent, describe such a moment and consider what it says about young children and the roles played by their teachers.

6. The next time you are with one or more young children, make a special effort to keep the improvisation mind-set alive. Afterward, write in a journal or tell others about how a more playful and spontaneous way of relating to children affected you as well as the child.

"Making Sense of Outdoor Pretend Play"/*Jane P. Perry*

Jane P. Perry, a research coordinator and teacher, directs readers' attention to the independent pretend play children engage in when outdoors. She suggests ways adults can set the stage for richer use of outdoor play environments.

7. Many public schools are shortening or even eliminating recess to make more time for academic subjects. On the basis of this article, what arguments can you make in support of outdoor play?

8. Many of us have vivid memories of outdoor play, whether we grew up in a city, the suburbs, or the country. Share some of your memories with fellow students or co-workers. What do these memories tell you about the contributions of outdoor play to development and learning?

9. Perry describes three phases or patterns of outdoor play: initiation, negotiation, and enactment. She also shares five guidelines for conducting "nonjudgmental observations" (p. 21). Try applying Perry's five guidelines while observing children at play. Watch to see how children move through the initiation, negotiation, and enactment phases. In what ways can you help them progress in their play?

10. Some teachers have negative feelings about the outdoors (e.g., they find it too hot or too cold, see outdoor play as a time for their own break, or dislike dirt and bugs). Such feelings can influence whether and how they support children's outdoor play. Examine your own feelings about the outdoors. How do your feelings enhance or discourage children's play and learning while outdoors?

"Playing to Get Smart"/*Elizabeth Jones*

In this Viewpoint article, Elizabeth (Betty) Jones, noted author and teacher educator, makes a strong case for why children play—to "get smart." However, her definition of getting smart goes far beyond rote learning.

11. If you agree with Betty Jones's definition of getting smart through play, you might share with others the validity of these views. Use photos or anecdotes from your observations to show how children develop creativity, critical thinking, and social problem solving through flexible, imaginative play.

12. Jones gives an example of a teacher "rescuing" pretend play that is beginning to fall apart by imaginatively entering the play with a new role and some new ideas. Try this strategy, and then share your experience with others.

13. Jones shares an example of teachers brainstorming curriculum opportunities that could come from collecting shells at the beach. With staff in your program or fellow students, pick a topic, then brainstorm and "web" the rich curriculum possibilities that might emerge as children play with ordinary materials and engage in everyday activities.

"Play: Children's Context for Development"/*Tovah P. Klein, Daniele Wirth, and Keri Linas*

The authors, teachers of adults and children, illustrate the defining characteristics of play—positive affect, active engagement, intrinsic motivation, freedom from external rules, attention to process, and non-literality. They discuss the teacher's role in facilitating and supporting play and include practical suggestions for teachers.

14. How do you know when it's really play? Sharpen your observation skills by using the authors' list of the defining characteristics of play. Consider them as you watch a child in the classroom or outdoors. It might be helpful to devise a checklist using the authors' criteria.

15. The authors' vignettes paint vivid pictures of the characteristics and the value of play. Think about the children you know best, and then write several such examples to share with other adults.

16. The authors provide suggestions for how teachers can support and facilitate children's play. From this list, identify one that you would especially like to focus on in your own teaching. Emphasize this skill in your classroom for a week—ideally with help from a fellow teacher or mentor—and share your experiences with others.

"Thanks for the Memory: The Lasting Value of True Play"/*David Elkind*

David Elkind, author, educator, and former NAEYC president, argues that play is valuable not just because it helps children learn, but also because it creates joy and enduring, comforting memories.

17. Elkind begins by summarizing several theories about the meaning and value of play—each one developed from an adult's point of view. Which of these seems most convincing to you? Which seems most consistent with your personal or professional experiences?

18. The *Reader's Digest* article referred to by Elkind, "The Day We Flew the Kites," describes one play experience still recalled by community members many years later. Write, draw, or tell about a memorable play experience in your life—or ask older family members to share their memories.

"Play Modifications for Children with Disabilities"/*Susan R. Sandall*

Children with disabilities have the right to experience the joy and value of play. Illustrating her suggestions with examples, Susan R. Sandall describes a variety of play adaptations and modifications.

19. Sandall recommends beginning by observing carefully to learn which play activities interest a child who has a disability, and then planning how to modify the activity to include the child. In your early childhood program, try this observation/planning process and share the results with colleagues.

20. Many of Sandall's suggestions would also be helpful for children who do not have disabilities but who may have difficulty getting involved in play for other reasons, such as shyness or language differences. Select one of the modifications and use it to increase the play engagement of a child you know.

"Beyond Banning War and Superhero Play: Meeting Children's Needs in Violent Times"/*Diane E. Levin*

Teachers struggle with how to deal with children's fascination with violent play themes. Diane E. Levin, teacher educator and expert on promoting healthy development in violent times, shares her ideas about where this fascination comes from and how teachers can address children's needs.

21. Like most teachers, you probably know at least one child whose fascination with violent play themes has created concerns. You might write about or describe this child in light of Levin's ideas.

22. From Levin's suggested approaches to working with children's violent play, choose one or two to implement in your classroom or student teaching experiences. After several weeks, share your experiences with others.

23. Many parents—and teachers—think that any form of war play or other violent play should be banned from early childhood classrooms. Levin suggests a different approach. If, after reading this article, you choose to permit this type of play in your classroom, how might you explain your decision to families or administrators?

"Learning to Play Again: A Constructivist Workshop for Adults"/*Ingrid Chalufour, Walter F. Drew, and Sandra Waite-Stupiansky*

Does play benefit adults too? The authors, who are experienced teacher educators, describe hands-on play workshops that help teachers construct their knowledge about play by connecting their play experiences with those of young children.

24. In your daily life, do you have opportunities for play? If so, what value do you find in play? If not, how might you restore play to your life?

25. In the play workshops, adults experience three forms of play: solitary, parallel, and cooperative. What is the value of each of these play types—for adults as well as for children?

26. Design a play workshop for a group of adults—perhaps your co-workers or fellow students. If your workshop is for a shorter period, consider the effects of the time limit on people's ability to become fully involved in the play. Develop ways to evaluate reactions to the workshop and, if possible, effects on the adults' subsequent work with children.

27. Although adult play and children's play have some common elements, play serves a different role for young children than it does for adults. What are some of the similarities and differences between the play of children and that of adults? How might these similarities and differences affect your teaching practices?

C. Making connections

Consider the big picture

1. In your view, what are the three most important themes or key ideas that recur across this group of articles? Compare your nominations with those identified by other readers.

2. Again thinking of the entire group of articles, what are three key teacher behaviors that support young children's play? What three aspects of the indoor and outdoor environments do the same?

3. Because this is a small selection of articles, some important ideas may have been left out or under-represented. In your mind, what is missing in this discussion of play in the early childhood years? (Some examples are play in different periods of history, play therapy, assessment of play skills.) Where can you learn more about these missing topics?

Examine curriculum goals and expected outcomes

4. Read the following classroom descriptions from the revised edition of NAEYC's book, *Developmentally Appropriate Practice in Early Childhood Programs* (p. 128):

   • Teachers do not help children make good use of choice time. They rarely intervene when children do the same things over and over or become disruptive. Rather than assisting children in developing decision-making skills, teachers overuse time-out or use punishment to control disruptive children.

   • During children's play and choice activities, teachers assume a passive role, contributing little or nothing to children's play and learning.

   In these two examples, the teachers do not support meaningful play. What would you expect children to do in response to the teachers' actions or lack of involvement? Using what you have learned from the articles in this book, from your observations and discussions, and from your work with young children, what appropriate practices would you recommend that these teachers use to support, rather than discourage, children's play?

5. Many early childhood programs have adopted a specific curriculum model (for example, the Creative Curriculum for Early Childhood, the Montessori curriculum, the Reggio Emilia approach, the project approach, Tools of the Mind [the Vygotskian approach], the High/Scope curriculum). With other teachers or students, examine two or more of these models and compare how each curriculum incorporates play.

6. Most states now have early learning standards describing what young children should know and be able to do in the years before kindergarten. If your state has such standards, consider how a strongly play-focused program might help children develop knowledge and skills related to these standards. (To find your state's standards, visit the National Institute for Early Education Research at http://nieer.org/ and go to your state's databank; or check ELO Resources at the SERVE report Web site, www.serve.org/ELO/research.html.)

7. The Head Start Child Outcomes Framework presents building blocks that are important for school success. (The Framework is available online at www.headstartinfo.org/pdf/hsoutcomesguide final4c/pdf; see p. 10 of the Leader's Guide.) Review the Framework and, working with colleagues or fellow students, compare some of your state's expectations for young children's learning and development, as delineated in the state standards, with those of the Framework. What are major common elements and differences?

Use reflection to enhance teaching practices

8. As you read and discuss this entire set of articles, what do you find that affirms your current practices? What questions do the articles raise about your practices? What new approaches might you try?

9. Many of the authors emphasize that teachers should take an active approach to promoting "mature" or developmentally valuable play, rather than assuming that good play will occur without any adult intervention. What do you and your colleagues think about this idea? What risks or benefits do you see in this more activist role for teachers?

10. Although getting involved is important, there is also value in stepping back and just watching as children play. Besides observing children playing in child development programs and schools, you can observe children in other settings—on playgrounds, at the beach or park, at home, while waiting at a bus station or in a doctor's office. What new insights can you gain from looking at play in different settings?

11. While observing children's play, you have no doubt noticed that some children seem to be more skilled or capable players than others—more imaginative, better able to enter or lead or devise complex play scenarios. Based on ideas in this book, what might be some reasons for these differences, and how can you help children who lack play skills to develop them more fully?

12. Most of the articles in this book point out that children's play has many benefits besides the sheer joy of play—supporting learning, promoting language development, developing creativity, enhancing social competence, and so on. Using these articles, create an individual or group list of the many benefits of play, and share it with other staff

or families. Documentation with photographs would add to the impact of this list.

Focus on families and communities

13. Many families have understandable concerns about their children's future academic development. They may not value play or understand how it is linked to learning. Using examples from the articles in this collection, how could you help families better understand the role of play in supporting their children's development and learning?

14. With colleagues or fellow students, create kits of recycled, easily available, and free materials that families and children can play with together at home (along the lines of the teacher workshop described in the article by Chalufour, Drew, and Waite-Stupiansky). Develop a plan for making the kits and prepare a handout with suggestions. Be sure to adapt the authors' suggestions to the cultures and community that your program serves.

15. All adults, whatever their culture, community environment, or personal history, played when they were young. How might you encourage children's parents, grandparents, and other family members to share their own play memories? What would be the value in doing so?

16. All families love to see photographs of their children. How could you use photography or videos to help family members experience the wonders of their children's play? For example, you might create displays or documentation panels that pair photos of children's activities with quotes from the chil-dren describing their play activities; or during an evening family meeting, you might show videos of the children at play.

Identify resources and plan next steps

17. The **"Resources"** section (pp. 58–59) contains a rich menu of play-related books, articles, and Web sites. In addition, most articles have a list of references specific to that topic. Select one or more of these resources, and write an annotated description of it to guide others—perhaps putting the information in handouts or on a Web page. What is the early childhood content of the material? For which professionals is it especially valuable? For which children?

18. Besides those listed in this book, what other resources have you found to support your understanding of children's play and your ability to help children develop more mature and enjoyable play? Again, you might create an annotated list to share.

19. What do you think you need to learn to better support children's play? What will you change—in your classroom, your schedule, the outdoor play area, your teaching practices, and so on?

20. Develop specific plans to more fully engage the children in your class in imaginative, mature, joyful, and productive play—play both for its own sake and to foster other areas of competence. Create an action plan to guide this work. Implement your plans and record what happens through observation notes, journal entries, video, or photos.